HORIZONTAL JESUS

TONY EVANS

HARVEST HOUSE PUBLISHERS
EUGENE, OREGON

HORIZONTAL JESUS
Copyright © 2015 Tony Evans
Published by Harvest House Publishers
Eugene, Oregon 97402
www.harvesthousepublishers.com

Library of Congress Cataloging-in-Publication Data
Evans, Tony, 1949-
Horizontal Jesus / Tony Evans.
    pages cm
ISBN 978-0-7369-5899-8 (pbk.)
ISBN 978-0-7369-5900-1 (eBook)
1. Love—Religious aspects—Christianity. 2. Christian life. I. Title.
BV4639.E93 2015
241'.4—dc23

                                                         2015004973

Contents

Take a stroll down the yellow brick road as
Tony paints a word portrait of the critical part
we play in each other's lives.

GO.TONYEVANS.ORG/HJ

JESUS'S HANDS AND FEET

C an the things we do for others affect what God does for us—for better or for worse?

We might think the answer is no. God has saved us by grace through faith, not by our works. So how could what we do for others possibly affect what God does for us? Doesn't that sound legalistic, as if we could earn God's blessings? Besides, God is sovereign. He has a plan, and no one can prevent Him from accomplishing it. Surely a few small details—such as the way we treat other people—won't keep the God of all creation from doing what He has purposed to do, right? We can't influence the heart and hand of the sovereign God of the universe simply by the way we treat other people, can we?

Then again, maybe we can.

In fact, the answer from Scripture is a resounding *yes*. Our relationships with other people do affect our experience of God. Not because we can earn God's answers to our prayers (we can't), and not because God hasn't already decided what to do (He most surely has). His plan is never in jeopardy. Rather, the reason why our horizontal relationships with each other affect our vertical experience of God is simply this: That's how God designed it to be. This is His kingdom.

God is the one who decided that the way we interact with others impacts the way He will interact with us. This is His design for us.

//

God's love is pure, and His grace is great. The question is, how much of that love and grace will we experience in our own lives?

\\

God's love is pure, and His grace is great. The question is, how much of that love and grace will we experience in our own lives? God freely pours out His blessings, but we can receive them only if we allow them to flow through us and out to others.

Maybe an illustration will help us grasp this truth. I have four kids, and I love them dearly. My love for them is secure. They never need to worry about losing my love, and they never need to worry about no longer being my children. Each one will forever and always be my child.

However, when the kids were growing up, we had certain standards in our home—behavioral expectations of how they were to treat their parents and how they were to treat each other. When they broke these standards, we never stopped loving them. They never stopped being our children. But they did experience a different side of us.

For example, if one of my daughters was playing with a friend at our house, and if my other daughter wanted to join in, both of our girls knew that they were to be polite and inclusive as an act of love. They also knew there were consequences for the way they handled the situation. If my daughters treated each other with love and respect, they knew what to expect from me when I got home. But if they decided to snub each other and be rude and unkind, they knew they would experience another response from me when I arrived.

<hr/>

Just as any parent's heart aches when their children hurt one another, God's heart is burdened when that happens in the body of Christ.

<hr/>

This wasn't because I loved them any less. It wasn't because our relationship was severed—just the opposite. It was because my job as their father included training them and enforcing the relational expectations in our home. So if one daughter excluded the other, I would sit her down and explain that what she did was hurtful and wrong. And perhaps that night, she would not be included in family game time simply as a reminder of what it feels like to be left out. Again, my love for her hadn't changed. My role in her life as her father hadn't changed. But her actions changed her experience of me for that evening.

God is a loving Father, and He loves each of us passionately. Just as any parent's heart aches when their children hurt one another, God's heart is burdened when that happens in the body of Christ.

In addition, when God bestows His favor on each of us—good health, blessed finances, unique skills, or relational acumen—He doesn't do that simply for our own benefit. He does that so that we can be conduits of His blessings to others. When His blessings stop with us and don't flow through us to others, do you think He's going to continue pouring out His favor on us? What would you do with your child? Imagine you're in a candy store with two of your kids, and you decide to buy one bag of candy for them to share. You pay for the candy, hand the bag to the older child, and ask him to share it with your younger child. The older child is the steward of the candy, but he's not the owner. It belongs to both of them because it ultimately belongs to you.

Now imagine that your older child begins hoarding all the candy and refusing to give any to your younger child. What would you do? When the candy ran out, would you refill the bag with more candy and give it to your older child again? Or would you make other arrangements this time? Your love for your child wouldn't change. But your child's experience of your blessing and provision in his life would definitely change.

Similarly, none of us are owners of what we have—our time, talents, or treasures. These things all belong to God. He entrusts them to us so we can use them to advance His kingdom on earth, benefit one another, and glorify Him. When we don't align our actions with God's teaching on how we are to be with one another, we are not removing ourselves from God's family. We are not cutting ourselves off from Him. But we are limiting the full expression and experience of His presence and goodness in our lives—not because He is mean, but because He is good.

The aim of our lives is to reflect the image of our Creator.

When our son Jonathan was in training camp with the San Diego Chargers, my wife, Lois, and I flew to San Diego from time to time to watch him at the stadium or to visit him at his home. San Diego is a beautiful place, and we always enjoyed our visits. An interesting statue in San Diego is erected at Christ the King Church. The statue is of Jesus, but its hands are missing. As the story goes, vandals broke them off in the mid-1980s.

Rather than having the statue repaired, the pastor chose to put a plaque at the base of it that reads, "I have no hands but yours." It is declaring that because Jesus has ascended to His rightful place in the heavens and is not physically present on earth, we, His body, are to be His hands to one another. We are to be His feet to one another. We are to offer His help to one another. We are to live out our horizontal relationships with one another in light of our vertical relationship with Christ. We are to be the manifestation of Jesus to one another. That is our ultimate calling as His disciples. That is our highest aim and the truest reflection of the two greatest commands, "'Love the Lord your God with all your heart, and with all your soul, and with all your mind, and with all your strength'...[and] 'You shall love your neighbor as yourself'" (Mark 12:30-31).

No one knows for sure who wrote this poem, but it is widely attributed to Teresa of Avila, a sixteenth-century nun.

> Christ has no body but yours,
> No hands, no feet on earth but yours,
> Yours are the eyes with which he looks
> Compassion on this world,
> Yours are the feet with which he walks to do good,
> Yours are the hands with which he blesses all the world.
> Yours are the hands, yours are the feet,
> Yours are the eyes, you are his body.
> Christ has no body now but yours,
> No hands, no feet on earth but yours,
> Yours are the eyes with which he looks
> Compassion on this world.
> Christ has no body now on earth but yours.

The apostle Paul shares a similar sentiment in his letter to the church at Rome.

> How then will they call on Him in whom they have not believed? How will they believe in Him whom they have not heard? And how will they hear without a preacher? How will they preach unless they are sent? Just as it is written, "How beautiful are the feet of those who bring good news of good things!" (Romans 10:14-15).

We are to preach Jesus Christ in all that we do. As the common quote says, "Preach the gospel at all times. When necessary, use words."

The aim of our lives is to reflect the image of our Creator. He has given us good works to do (Ephesians 2:10). These involve treating others in certain ways. So by saying that what we do for others can affect what God does for us, we are affirming that our obedience to God's intended purpose in our lives can open up the floodgates of His ongoing blessing and favor. The converse of that is true as well— disobedience to His intended purpose can block the flow of His goodness to us.

Of course God is always free to give us grace, blessing, and favor regardless of what we do or don't do. This isn't a hard-and-fast rule. God can do whatever He wants, whenever He wants. We can never force His hand—but we can influence it.

Giving to others, then, influences your experience of God's blessings more than you may have realized. So do loving one another, serving one another, encouraging one another, and the like, as you'll discover in the pages of this book. We're going to look at several of the "one anothers" in Scripture—passages that show us how to be God's hands and feet, how to live as a horizontal Jesus, representing Him to those around us.

1

THE THEOLOGY OF "IT"

Have you ever given to others, only to feel as if you came out on the short end of the stick when all was said and done? Have you ever sacrificially helped someone or done something for God that you wouldn't want to do again because of what it cost you?

Sometimes we can be tempted to feel sorry for ourselves because of the things we have given up or the sacrifices we have made to follow Christ and represent Him as a horizontal Jesus to others. If you have experienced this, rest assured that you are not alone. Actually, you're in good company.

The disciples felt that way one day after Jesus challenged a rich man to sell his possessions and follow Him. The man decided to keep his wealth and walk away from Jesus. The disciples watched this, and then Peter spoke up: "Behold, we have left everything and followed You" (Mark 10:28). Was Peter feeling a little put-out because of all he'd given up to follow Christ? This was Jesus's response:

> Truly I say to you, there is no one who has left house or brothers or sisters or mother or father or children or farms, for My sake and for the gospel's sake, but that he

will receive a hundred times as much now in the present age, houses and brothers and sisters and mothers and children and farms, along with persecutions; and in the age to come, eternal life (verses 29-30).

In my Evans's paraphrase, Jesus was saying, "If you give away something or lose something because you are following Me and sharing Me with others, whatever you think you have lost, you will receive it back multiplied."

What you lose *for* God is returned
by God many times over.

Now, that's a very interesting promise. Some people have certainly abused it, turning God into a Santa Claus who gives us whatever we want as if He were obligated to meet all our demands and make us rich and successful. That error is often called prosperity theology, and it makes the material, physical world more important than the immaterial, spiritual domain. Jesus makes it clear that the motivation behind our ministry to others must be authentic, pure, and God-centered.

But let's not lose the power of Jesus's words. What you lose *for* God is returned *by* God many times over. Let's avoid both extremes. God is not a religious slot machine handing out goodies, but neither does He owe anything to anyone (Job 41:11). We must not fail to realize that what we do for others and give to them can affect what God does for and gives to us. This means we don't lose anything in living out our commitment to God without gaining it back—and often much more.

This brings us to Luke 6:38, which is the foundational verse for learning how live as a horizontal Jesus. In this verse Jesus lays out a strategic principle of giving and receiving. "Give, and it will be given to you. They will pour into your lap a good measure—pressed down, shaken together, and running over. For by your standard of measure it will be measured to you in return."

I hope I didn't lose you when you saw that the first word of this verse is "give." Stay with me because we are not going to focus on that word right now, but on another critical little word.

Source and Resource

Obviously, you can give something only if it's yours to give. If you don't have it, you can't give it—whatever "it" happens to be. So before we talk about Jesus's promise in Luke 6:38, let's make sure we understand this very fundamental principle: You only have one source, and that's God. You may have many resources or channels through which God can give you whatever He wants. But He is your only source.

You see, once you make something other than God your source, you have to look to that thing, depend on it, bank on it, count on it, and maybe even *bow* to it. Also, if you are trusting in anything or anyone other than God as your source, that person or thing can be taken away from you. So you are setting yourself up for heartache when you trust in anything other than God as your ultimate source.

Your local grocery store is not your source. The grocer doesn't grow the food; the store is merely a retailer. If your favorite grocery store closes, you can go to another one because a grocery store is not your source in the first place. It's merely a distribution center.

Your job is not the source of the income you need to live and pay your bills. Your job is important, but it too is merely a channel through which you receive. But what if your job *is* your source? If that's the case...well, if you lose your job, you lose everything. The beautiful thing about having God as your only source is that no other person or thing can own you or control you. That's why God calls us to fully depend on Him as our only source. He can switch secondary resources anytime or shift the method by which He delivers to you the things you need. But He remains your source.

So let me give you what I call the theology of "it" based on Jesus's promise in Luke 6:38. Whatever *it* is that you legitimately want or need from God, give it *to* God first—by giving it to someone else. Now, that's probably not what you usually hear, so stay with me as I show you what Jesus is teaching in Luke 6:38.

When in Need, Plant a Seed

Everybody wants something from God, but we saw in Mark 10:29-30 that Jesus reveals what comes first. When we give up houses or lands or family or anything else for the sake of Jesus and the gospel, we will receive a hundred times as much.

Whatever you plant, that is what you will receive back.

The theology of "it" is based on a principle God established in creation. "The earth brought forth vegetation, plants yielding seed after their kind, and trees bearing fruit with seed in them, after their kind; and God saw that it was good" (Genesis 1:12). Here's how the principle works. All the plants and trees that God created contained seeds so they could reproduce "after their kind." So whatever you plant, that is what you will receive back—after its own kind. You can't plant a pear seed and get watermelons.

This is the way God created life to work. If you want or need something, you first give it away by planting a seed. You take the seed from what you already have in order to replicate it.

Jesus broadened this principle of creation into a principle of life in Luke 6:38. Whatever you give, that's what you'll get back. God responds to your faith when you give away whatever it is that you need.

To put it another way, when you have a particular need, make sure you sow that particular kind of seed into other people's lives. Don't just ask God to meet your need without making sure you plant the same kind of seed.

Let's say Farmer Brown wants to have a good crop of fruit and vegetables on his ten acres. In fact, Farmer Brown is so serious about this that he stands in his field every day and prays, "God, I need You to bless my farm. I need rain, sunshine, and no bad weather so I can have a great harvest. In fact, God, I'm so serious about my need that I'm going to fast, go to church, and study my Bible. I want You to know I am really committed because I need You to bless the productivity of my farm."

We would say Farmer Brown is serious about God meeting his need. But what if we found out Farmer Brown never bothered to plant any seed? All of his efforts would be wasted because he was asking God to meet his need without planting any seed.

Remember the principle of Genesis 1:12? What God will do for us is tied not only to our need but also to the seed. God requires us to plant the seed. Why? So we will always know that our source is God, who created the ground and who sends the rain and sunshine that make the crop grow. And to remind us that the crop is to benefit others, not just ourselves.

I want you to understand the theology of "it" because it shows how God wants to meet many of your needs—assuming you're willing to do something with the "it" He has given to you. No farmer eats everything he produces because his future is built into the seed. We can observe this principle in operation in Scripture.

Faith Is a Function

One example involves a widow of Zarephath (1 Kings 17:8-16) who was trying to survive a drought. When the prophet Elijah met her and asked her for some water and bread, she told him she only had enough flour and oil for one cake of bread. She and her son were going to share it and then starve to death. This woman had a desperate need for food, but what did Elijah tell her to do? Make him a cake of bread first. Then he gave her this promise: "For thus says the LORD God of Israel, 'The bowl of flour shall not be exhausted, nor shall the jar of oil be empty, until the day that the LORD sends rain on the face of the earth'" (verse 14).

Faith is acting out your conviction
that God is telling the truth.

This widow could have said, "You don't understand; I only have enough for one cake." But God was saying to her, "I know you have a need, but I want you to plant a seed by feeding My prophet." So the widow gave the very thing she needed, and *it*—the bread—came back to her in such abundance that she and her son had more than enough to get them through the drought. This widow planted a seed by giving God something to work with. That's called faith.

Faith is acting out your conviction that God is telling the truth.

It's making choices that reflect your belief that God is trustworthy. Faith is not a feeling—it's a function. So when you come to God with a need, He has two questions: "What do you need Me to give you?" and "How are you giving it to others?"

We find another example of this principle at work in the Old Testament book of 1 Samuel. A woman named Hannah and her husband, Elkanah, had been married for years, but Hannah was unable to conceive. In her culture, infertility was not only an emotional burden but also a social stigma and a financial liability. Her shame and disappointment compounded her need to get pregnant.

When Hannah went before the Lord to express her need for a child, she practiced the theology of "it." The very thing she needed—a child—was the very thing she vowed to give back to God.

> She made a vow and said, "O LORD of hosts, if You will indeed look on the affliction of Your maidservant and remember me, and not forget Your maidservant, but will give Your maidservant a son, then I will give him to the LORD all the days of his life" (1 Samuel 1:11).

The "it" Hannah wanted was a son, and that's exactly what she was willing to give back. God heard her prayer and answered her by giving her a son. She named him Samuel, and when he was old enough, she took him to live in the temple and minister to the Lord, just as she said she would.

> [Hannah] would make him a little robe and bring it to him from year to year when she would come up with her husband to offer the yearly sacrifice. Then Eli [the priest] would bless Elkanah and his wife and say, "May the LORD give you children from this woman in place of the one she dedicated to the LORD." And they went to their own home.

The Lord visited Hannah; and she conceived and gave
birth to three sons and two daughters (1 Samuel 2:19-21).

Hannah's empty quiver became full when she gave back to God
(and by extension, to the people of Israel) the very thing she needed
and had asked for.

In one of the most beautiful stories in the Bible, Ruth, a young
widow in need of security, gave her aging mother-in-law security by
promising never to leave her. As a result, Ruth later received the security of a relationship with a husband—Boaz.

Give, and *it* will be given to you.

We see the same principle at work in the New Testament as well
when we come across a crowd of more than 5000 men (plus women
and children) who had been following Jesus for several days and were
hungry. As the people began to complain of hunger and the disciples
began to fret about what to do, Jesus asked them how they were going
to feed so many. The crowd needed food, so Jesus asked the disciples
to find some food.

The disciples searched, but all they could find was a young boy
with some sardines and crackers (John 6:9). It was exactly what they
needed, but it was not nearly enough—and it was also the little boy's
lunch! We often overlook the fact that this little boy was no doubt
hungry himself. For him to give up his lunch was no small sacrifice.
And yet he gave to Jesus the very thing that the people needed—food.

When Jesus received *it* (the gift of food), He blessed it, gave thanks
to God, and turned *it* into enough food to feed everyone with plenty
left over. By giving up his lunch, the little boy had planted a seed,
and Jesus turned it into an overabundance of food. The boy surely
received more than he had given.

The widow of Zarephath, Hannah, Ruth, and this young boy
were each like a horizontal Jesus to those around them. They were

willing to give—even when they didn't seem to have enough them-selves—so that others could gain. As a result, they received tremen-dous blessings too.

///

When God sees our faith demonstrated
in our feet, He responds.

\\\

Unfortunately, some people want God to manufacture a miracle even though they aren't willing to plant a seed by giving away what they have. This usually means one of two things. Either they aren't motivated to glorify God and advance His kingdom, or they aren't exercising any faith at all. But when God sees our faith demonstrated in our feet, He responds.

So if you want to be forgiven, give forgiveness. If you need love, give love. If you need a promotion on your job, give extra at the office and seek the welfare of your coworkers. You could even promote someone else, such as a neighbor's kid who wants to raise money by mowing lawns. If you want to grow spiritually, invest in the spiritual growth of others. Whatever *it* is you need, give it away so it can be returned to you. The solution to your need is in the seed when you plant it as an expression of your faith in God and obedience to Him.

I don't know about you, but as I was studying and learning about this principle, I wanted to go out and minister to anyone I ran into! I'd look at my life, identify a need, and then go find someone with a similar need and minister to them, confident that I would see God supply what I needed.

But keep in mind that we don't give just so we can get something in return. We're motivated by our love for God and for other people, not by greed and selfishness. God is sovereign, and He alone knows what is ultimately the best for us. We can't demand that He meet our terms. We are in a loving relationship with God, not a business deal.

The "it" in Luke 6:38 refers to an action of ministering to someone; it's not just about money or things. Likewise, God's principle of "it" has to do with our heart, our motivation. It's not giving to get. Rather, it's giving to serve. Giving to minister to someone. As you give from a pure heart to truly minister to someone else as an expression of your love for God, He sees your heart and then gives you what you need. It's a subtle yet critical difference.

God's Abundant Giving

Look at Luke 6:38 again. Jesus said, "They" will pour out a blessing to you. Who are "they"? They are whoever God chooses to use to meet your need. God has a supply of need meeters that He can call on to bless seed planters.

Jesus continued, "They will pour into your lap a good measure—pressed down, shaken together, and running over." To understand what Jesus is saying, you need to think agriculturally. Jesus was speaking about grain.

In New Testament days, a person would go to a merchant and ask for a certain measure of wheat. The merchant would scoop out the measure the person ordered, but the merchant would put only about three-fourths of the full measure in the buyer's bag. Then he would shake the buyer's sack to let the contents settle before adding the rest of the grain so the buyer would get his full order without any gaps. And then the merchant would press down on the grain to create room for more.

Jesus referenced this common practice to illustrate the abundance of God's giving. And He took it to another level by saying that God keeps pouring His blessing into your sack until it's running over.

God says when you give "it" (whatever you need) to others—serving as a horizontal Jesus—He uses them to meet your need. They give to you what you gave away. And when God does this, He creates room for more. This excites me because it's based on our relationship with Him and our service to others. It's not a way to get what we want.

This principle also helps to explain why so many of us believers are not seeing more evidence of God showing up on every level in our lives. God doesn't appear to be showing up experientially in our vertical relationship with Him because we are refusing to give practically in our horizontal relationships with others. The problem is that we want God to meet our needs, but we're not willing to give to anyone else.

A lot of Christians want to be blessed, but they don't want to give more of themselves—their time, talents, and treasures—to God for the benefit of others. They want their needs met in the pressed-down, shaken-together way Jesus described in Luke 6:38 without fulfilling the principles and precepts of the "one another" passages of Scripture. Being a conduit for blessing is critical to experiencing true blessing from God.

The Standard of Measure

Jesus brings the point home in the last statement of this verse: "For by your standard of measure it will be measured to you in return." If you give God only a thimble to fill, that's all you will get back in return.

God wants followers who are conduits, not cul-de-sacs.

This is the secret to the kind of blessing in your vertical experience of God I have been talking about. Look at this command God gave the Israelites through Moses:

> When you reap your harvest in your field and have forgotten a sheaf in the field, you shall not go back to get it; it shall be for the alien, for the orphan, and for the widow, in order that the LORD your God may bless you in all the work of your hands (Deuteronomy 24:19).

God says when you leave part of your crop for the needy—when you plant a seed for others—He will bless *you*. That's just one of several clear, biblical pictures of how our horizontal relationship with others can affect our vertical experience of God.

Remember, a blessing is not only what God does *for* you but also what He is free to do *through* you. God told Abraham, "I will bless those who bless you...and all peoples on earth will be blessed through you" (Genesis 12:3 NIV).

This is why Jesus said, "It is more blessed to give than to receive" (Acts 20:35). When God knows He can flow through you horizontally, His blessings will freely flow to you vertically. But the moment God sees that it's only about you, that His blessings are going to stop with you and not flow through you to someone else, He is not as interested in continuing the flow of His blessings to you. He wants followers who are conduits, not cul-de-sacs.

This is one of the primary reasons you need to intentionally plug in to a local body of believers. The church is the key context, outside of your family, where you can live out the Bible's "one anothers" because He wants us to minister to His spiritual family.

In any context, you can give "it" to God by giving "it" to others, and "it" will flow back to you, poured out in blessing. This promise is not limited to your finances, but applies to any area of need, including encouragement, love, and healing.

I want to close this chapter by looking at a very familiar verse. Many of us have quoted it throughout the years but without fully understanding its context. It's found in Philippians 4:19, and you may already know it by heart. "My God will supply all your needs according to His riches in glory in Christ Jesus." Everyone I know loves this verse! And what's not to love? God is promising to meet our needs according to His riches in glory.

However, when you read the preceding verses in Philippians 4, you'll see the "it" principle at work. God's promise to meet your needs is not unconditional. Rather, it came to people who were meeting others' needs first.

> No church shared with me in the matter of giving and receiving but you alone...Not that I seek the gift itself, but I seek for the profit which increases to your account. But I have received everything in full and have an abundance; I am amply supplied, having received from Epaphroditus what you have sent, a fragrant aroma, an acceptable sacrifice, well-pleasing to God (verses 15,17-18).

Before Paul writes his famous words about God supplying all the Philippians' needs, he acknowledges that they had already met his needs. He called their gifts an "acceptable sacrifice, well-pleasing to God." The "it" he said they would receive (God meeting their needs) came as a result of the "it" they had given (them meeting someone else's needs first). Unfortunately we often miss that and skip straight to Philippians 4:19, only to think God has come up short when He fails to meet all of our needs. Or we sometimes give very little but expect a lot from God. Remember, in Luke 6:38 we are told, "By your standard of measure it will be measured to you in return."

God's promises are oftentimes conditional—their fulfillment may depend on the state of our heart and extent of our obedience. This isn't a truth we always like to discuss, but that doesn't make it any less true. If you will embrace this reality, if you will begin to see the things you do and give to others as investments in your relationship with God, you will reap the fruit of your labor. God's promises are good, and He stands by them. But they often require acts of faith, for without faith it's impossible to please Him (Hebrews 11:6).

In the next several chapters, I'm going to walk with you through several "one another" teachings in Scripture. This is the best way to see how our Lord desires for you to live—as a horizontal Jesus to those around you.

2

THE LAW OF THE HARVEST

Across the street from our sanctuary in Dallas is our education center, the largest and most expensive facility on our campus. It gives us the space and technology we need to hold a huge variety of programs—not only ministries for children and youth but also many opportunities for adults.

Some time ago, however, we encountered a major problem in this center. People entering on the east side of the building were being hit with a putrid smell, and they quickly let us know that something was wrong. We had a dilemma. Despite the size and cost of this building, and despite all the programs we held there, it wasn't fulfilling its intended purpose.

We brought in professionals to find out why this valuable facility had such an offensive odor. They discovered that a pipe from one of the restrooms was cracked and leaking. In addition, the fan designed to vent the bathroom was actually turning the wrong way, pushing the odor back down into the building instead of lifting it out. Until the problems were solved and the atmosphere was cleared, a facility that was designed for good was being contaminated by something bad.

There's a lesson here for us. Your church building or your house cannot fulfill its intended purpose if it is contaminated by faulty spiritual, relational, or emotional connections. It doesn't matter how much that building costs. It doesn't matter how much money you spend on plans and programs or how carefully you lay out your calendar. Until the reason for the "odor" is addressed, what was designed for good will be contaminated.

The church is a community where real people in real relationships are meeting real needs in real ways.

God created the church to be an environment that fosters healthy spiritual family relationships. It's to be a place where people can live out authentic Christianity. However, far too often the church has become a place of unwanted odors. These stem from unhealthy relationships, selfishness, laziness, legalism, and more. In the same way, our homes, which were designed to be places where we receive solace, comfort, and peace, are far too often places of war. Most of the issues and odors we face stem from disobedience to God's commands to treat one another in certain ways. On the other hand, when we treat one another in the manner that God directs us to, our relationships, small groups, workplaces, homes, and the like become pleasing to all of us.

God wants the church to be a community where real people in real relationships are meeting real needs in real ways. God did not create the church simply as a classroom where you get instruction or as a theater where you come to watch a performance.

This vision for our life together sounds great, but making it a reality takes work. Too often we in the church are like the cutout figures you find at a carnival. The body of a beauty queen or a muscleman has the face cut out so people can stick their own heads in and have their pictures taken as if they were that person. But it doesn't take a genius to see that the face and the body don't go together.

We can run into that problem spiritually. Jesus is the head of the body, which is His church. But too often the head and the body don't appear to belong together. The apostle Paul has an answer for that problem in Romans 12:9-13.

Love Without Masks

Paul begins this section by saying: "Let love be without hypocrisy. Abhor what is evil; cling to what is good" (verse 9). True biblical love is *compassionately and righteously pursuing the well-being of another*.

The word translated "hypocrisy" comes from the ancient Greek theater. There weren't enough actors to play all the parts, so the actors played multiple characters by holding masks over their faces. Those actors were called *hypokritēs*, so you can see how this word came to mean someone who isn't sincere, someone who is simply pretending. We say he or she is wearing a mask. Paul says, "Don't love with a mask on." In other words, don't just play the part. The tragedy is that some of the best actors and actresses you'll ever see are in church because they come with a mask on.

Why do people wear masks, even among believers? Because they are afraid that if they unmask themselves and reveal who they really are, others will critique and criticize them. We all want to be loved, appreciated, and valued. Nothing is wrong with that. But none of us are perfect, so we often feel as if we have to wear a mask to hide our flaws so people will appreciate us. But when we do that, we have fallen into the trap of playing the hypocrite.

Here's the problem with wearing the mask. When we are not real with God, others, and ourselves, when we are trying to hide who we are, we are operating in the dark. The Bible says, "God is Light, and in Him there is no darkness at all. If we say that we have fellowship with Him and yet walk in the darkness, we lie and do not practice the truth" (1 John 1:5-6). Light exposes and darkness conceals, so when we live in the dark, we end up lying to God, to others, and to ourselves.

Paul set the biblical standard in Romans 12:9—for Christians to love without hypocrisy, without masks. Then Paul provides some definition to this kind of love: "Abhor what is evil; cling to what is good." That is, biblical love doesn't gloss over evil or ignore good. It calls wrong, wrong and right, right because love doesn't negate the truth. The body of Christ is to be an environment where you and I can love and be loved without wearing a mask or feeling the need to perform. It is to be an authentic environment for truth.

A Devoted Family

Paul continues his admonition in Romans 12 by saying, "Be devoted to one another in brotherly love; give preference to one another in honor." The word translated "brotherly love" refers to love in the context of a family. The word translated "devoted" means to be committed to one another.

This is not a description of casual relationships. There is no thought in the Bible of the church as a place of casual contact and surface relationships. No, Paul says the church is to be a place where we are devoted to each other in love, like members of a close-knit family. It's where people can live in the same spiritual house, which is why 1 Peter 4:17 calls the church "the household of God." God wants His children to be devoted to one another so we can benefit one another.

Children in an earthly family sometimes have to learn this lesson of mutual devotion and benefit the hard way. One day when my daughter Chrystal was an older teenager, she and I were at odds with each other. It was clear that we were not on the same page on the issue and that she was not going to back down. She folded her arms, gave me a grunt, and walked off.

I said, "Where do you think you're going?"

"I'm going to my room," she replied.

"*Your* room?" I said. "No, you're going to one of *my* rooms, and I let you sleep in it." Chrystal had never offered to pay any utilities or buy any food. Her name wasn't on the mortgage. But like many teenagers, she went to her room and shut the door as if nobody else lived in the house.

A lot of people relate to the church the way a teenager sometimes relates to his family.

Now, it's interesting that even though teenagers want their own room and their own space, they will come out and interact with the family when they want something. They want to raid the refrigerator for food they didn't pay for, or they want gas money or the keys to the car they didn't buy. Children like to think they are self-sufficient, but the fact is, they are part of a family and need to be devoted to their brothers and sisters in love. Sometimes kids need a wake-up call to that reality.

So do many people in the church. A lot of people relate to the church the way a teenager sometimes relates to his family—selfishly, "me first." They're like the man who went into a church one day and asked the pastor for financial help to pay his bills because he heard the church had an assistance program.

The pastor asked this man, "What church are you a part of?"

He replied, "Well, I'm part of the invisible church," which meant he wasn't attending a local church.

The pastor answered, "Well, okay. Here's some invisible money."

People like this guy seem to think, "The church is here just for me—and only when I need help." Well, if the Christian life included only God and me, I could stay home and live that way. But God calls you and me into community because we belong to something bigger than ourselves. God wants to make it crystal clear that our vertical relationship with Him includes our horizontal relationship with other believers.

Blessed to Be a Blessing

This means that a lot of what God wants to do with, in, and through you is not just for you. He wants it to flow out from you to benefit others. So if nothing is going out through your life to others horizontally, you may well be limiting what flows into your life from God vertically. The truth is that we are always blessed to be a blessing.

Here's my paraphrase of what Paul is saying in Romans 12:10: "I want you to be searching for opportunities to impact somebody outside of yourself." Now, you may be saying, "Why should I go to all the trouble of searching for someone else to help when I've got so much stuff going on in my life and could use some help myself?" The answer is that God pays attention to your horizontal responses to others when He gets ready to move vertically in your life. When you want something to come to you, reach out beyond yourself to someone else, because when you do, you get God's attention. The best way to get God to move on your behalf is to let Him see you moving on behalf of someone else.

Too many times we are like the man who sat down to lunch one day with his friend. They each ordered a filet of sole, but the waiter brought the two pieces of fish out on the same plate. One piece was bigger than the other, so the first guy took the smaller piece of fish and put it on his friend's plate, keeping the bigger piece for himself.

His friend got a little ticked off at the guy's selfishness and said, "Hey, wait a minute! What do you think you're doing?"

The first man replied, "What do you mean? What are you mad about?"

"You gave me the small piece and kept the big piece for yourself," his friend answered. "If it had been me, I would have given you the big piece and taken the small piece for myself."

"Well," the first guy said, "that's the way it worked out. So why are you complaining?"

That's not what the Bible means by preferring one another in love.

Life in the Fast Lane

Paul's line of thought in Romans 12 continues with a series of exhortations. He begins by saying we are to be "not lagging behind in diligence, fervent in spirit, serving the Lord" (verse 11). Some people have children who lag behind. They tell the kids to do something, and the children sort of do it in slow motion, as if they aren't really very excited about obeying.

Lagging behind means moving slowly when you ought to be moving fast. It means you're in the slow lane when you ought to be in the fast lane, serving the Lord and others. Paul says we need to be fervent in our service, which means to boil over. God wants you not only to impact other people but also to put it on hot. He wants you to go for it rather than just throwing something out there. To put it another way, when God benefits you so you can benefit others, don't say, "I'll do it next week or next month." Why? Because by then you'll cool off. You'll lose that boiling sense of urgency to do what needs to be done—what God wants to be done.

Don't miss the importance of the last phrase in verse 11—"serving the Lord." You can be fervent in reaching out to others because you are not only doing it for their benefit. You are also getting God's attention because you're serving Him. Remember, your horizontal relationships with others affect your vertical experience with God.

Paul continues in Romans 12, "Rejoicing in hope, persevering in tribulation, devoted to prayer, contributing to the needs of the saints, practicing hospitality" (verses 12-13). Caring for the needs of our fellow saints has to do with meeting needs among folks you know personally. In Scripture, "hospitality" usually refers to helping strangers. In particular, Paul exhorted believers in that day to welcome visiting preachers and missionaries, who often had nowhere else to stay (Romans 16:2; Philippians 2:29; Colossians 4:10). So the strangers were not just people off the street, but fellow believers who were not yet known to their hosts.

There is no doubt that the vertical and the horizontal dimensions of the Christian life interact with and impact one another. The more I look at this principle, the more I am struck by its importance. If we fail to love one another horizontally, carrying out God's "one another" commands and precepts, we are not going to experience everything God wants to do in our vertical experience of Him. A lot of Christians are hindering the flow of God's blessing by focusing only on themselves. Our lives must have an outward (horizontal) focus if we are to fully receive the upward (vertical) experience of God.

When we are each living as a horizontal Jesus to those around us, God explodes onto the scene.

To join a church is not merely to have a place to sit on Sunday. It is to build a community with other believers. This is what God is after, so authentic churches create healthy environments in which God is free to move. Regardless of how much money we spend or how many programs we come up with, if the church's environment is not conducive to growing and serving each other, God is not free to express all that He wants to do. But when the environment changes so that we are each living as a horizontal Jesus to those around us, God explodes onto the scene.

This principle is found in His law of love. The laws in God's Word are like the laws He has established in nature. The law of gravity says that what goes up must come down. Now, you don't have to like the law of gravity, but it rules anyway. Just jump off the top of a building and you'll see.

God's laws differ from His miracles in that a miracle occurs when God overrides His natural laws, such as when Jesus took five loaves and two small fish and created enough food to feed 15,000 to 20,000 people. You need to understand that miracles are the exception, not the rule. This was true even in Bible times. God broke through and did some miraculous things, but those miracles were not His normal way of operating.

The norm is that God operates within the rules or laws He has built into creation. I mention this because when it comes to God's law of love, many people pray for God to miraculously provide for their needs while skipping God's law to first love Him and love one another.

In chapter 1, we looked at Luke 6:38: "Give, and it will be given to you. They will pour into your lap a good measure—pressed down, shaken together, and running over. For by your standard of measure it will be measured to you in return." Jesus was presenting what we could call another law—the law of giving and getting. This teaches that the "it" you need is the "it" you are to give because when you obey the law of giving, God returns it to you in abundant measure. That's the way God normally works.

The Law of the Harvest

Another of God's laws is what I'm calling the law of the harvest. This law is really a continuation of what we studied in chapter 1, and you need to understand it because this is how things normally work in God's economy. Paul explains the law of the harvest in 2 Corinthians 9:6-15. I actually want to start with the last verse in this passage because it tells us why this law is important and sets the preceding verses in their proper context. Verse 15 says, "Thanks be to God for His indescribable gift!" Whatever this gift is, you can't describe it. Paul said he didn't have the vocabulary to sufficiently describe this gift because it is awesome beyond description.

Now, if a gift is that good, I want to know about it. So what is this gift that the Bible says is indescribable? We don't have to wonder because the answer is right there in our passage. "God is able to make all grace abound to you, so that always having all sufficiency in everything, you may have an abundance for every good deed" (verse 8).

The gift that God has given to each one of us, the gift that is beyond Paul's ability to articulate, is the gift of grace. Grace is the doctrine that separates Christianity from every other religion ever known to mankind. All other religions teach a form of works to earn salvation. Only Christianity teaches that salvation is a gift of God completely apart from anything we can do to earn it. In fact, God pours out His grace on us in spite of our sins and failures.

Now, *that's* a magnificent gift! Paul even enhances his description in verse 14 when he calls it God's "surpassing grace." If you are a believer, you have been given a gift that will blow your natural mind.

You need to understand that grace also operates according to God's laws. In 2 Corinthians 9, grace appears in the context of the law of the harvest, or the law of sowing and reaping. And if we are to enjoy the harvest of God's blessings, we need to know how to gain access to His grace. If we don't know what grace is or how to receive it, we won't be able to maximize the gift of grace we have been given.

My children gave me an iPad several years ago for Christmas. Now, I'm a paper-and-pencil kind of guy. But suddenly, I had a gift that would record and remember things for me and take pictures for me. This gift also had apps—something I never had on my yellow pad. If I need a flashlight, I have a flashlight app. If I want to keep stuff in file folders, there's an app for that. There's even an app that lets me play Ping-Pong without a table. I mean, this gift has all sufficiency in everything for every good deed.

The problem is, I'm used to doing things the old way. So even though I now have indescribable resources and power at my fingertips, I wind up just tinkering with my gift instead of maximizing it. That's how many of us believers are with God's indescribable gift of grace, which puts the inexhaustible supply of God's goodness at our fingertips.

Accessing the Vertical Flow of God's Grace

Accessing the vertical flow of God's grace is no small thing simply because grace is no small thing. In Ephesians 2:7, Paul says God saved us "so that in the ages to come He might show the surpassing riches of His grace in kindness toward us in Christ Jesus." My own Evans paraphrase reads, "You ain't seen nuthin' yet!" The phrase "the ages to come" is a reference to the endless ages of eternity, which means that God will continue to reveal new aspects of His grace throughout eternity.

But in order to tap into this inexhaustible supply of grace, you have to access it vertically. Now, don't misunderstand. This does not negate at all what I have just said about grace being freely given to you in Christ. Your sin has been fully paid for in Christ, which opens the door for you to receive God's favor. But in order for God's amazing grace to have meaning to you, you must access the grace that Jesus Christ delivered to a sinful race on the cross. You can't earn grace, but you need to access it.

Think of your relationship with your electric company. The electricity supplied to your house gives you all the power you need to operate any appliance or turn on the lights. But the electric company is not going to come over to switch on the lights in your home or plug in your appliances. The power is there because the electric company has given you the power to access it. But accessing it is up to you.

The same is true for the unlimited supply of grace God has made available to you. And here's the good news: Unlike the bill for your access to electricity, the bill for your access to grace has already been paid.

Let's plug this truth of God's marvelous grace back into our text in 2 Corinthians 9. I'll leave the verse numbers in the quote below because I want you to notice that Paul's statement about grace in verse 8 is sandwiched between verses 6-7 and 9-10, which talk about how to access grace in relationship to the law of the harvest.

> [6]Now this I say, he who sows sparingly will also reap sparingly, and he who sows bountifully will also reap bountifully. [7]Each one must do just as he has purposed in his

heart, not grudgingly or under compulsion, for God loves a cheerful giver. [8]And God is able to make all grace abound to you, so that always having all sufficiency in everything, you may have an abundance for every good deed; [9]as it is written, "He scattered abroad, He gave to the poor, His righteousness endures forever." [10]Now He who supplies seed to the sower and bread for food will supply and multiply your seed for sowing and increase the harvest of your righteousness.

These verses relate God's laws about giving and getting to a farming context. I refer to this sowing and reaping as the law of the harvest. If you understand farming, you'll understand how to access God's grace vertically through what you do horizontally.

The Rules of the Harvest

I want to give you six rules of the harvest from 2 Corinthians 9.

1. Your harvest depends on *whether* you sow. Verse 6 says, "He who sows..." This may seem obvious. You never hear a farmer say, "I'm hoping to get my harvest first." But a lot of people come to church asking God to bless them with a harvest from unsown seeds.

A farmer cannot harvest a crop without sowing the seed. As I said in chapter 1, Farmer Brown can stand in his field all day and ask God to bless him with a harvest. But unless Farmer Brown has planted his seed, his prayers will do no good. So if you have a need, the question is, did you plant a seed? Without the seed, the rain can fall and the sun can shine, but nothing is going to happen. If we want to experience God's grace, we must access it.

2. Your harvest depends on *what* you sow. This is the simple principle of farming that if you plant apple seeds, you won't get pear trees. You

have to plant the same thing you want to harvest. That's why Jesus said in Luke 6:38, "Give, and *it* will be given to you." Your need will tell you the kind of seed to plant so that your seed will reproduce after its own kind. The Bible cautions us, "Do not be deceived, God is not mocked; for whatever a man sows, this he will also reap" (Galatians 6:7).

Sow horizontally what you want to reap vertically.

The problem is, a lot of people want to sow selfishness and reap goodness. But if you sow evil, expect to reap evil unless you replant. To access God's grace in the law of the harvest, sow horizontally what you want to reap vertically.

3. Your harvest depends on *how much* you sow. Second Corinthians 9:6 continues, "He who sows sparingly will also reap sparingly, and he who sows bountifully will also reap bountifully." Do you know anyone who wants to do a little bit of work but take home a big paycheck? In the same way, some people want a big blessing from God, but they don't want to actively cooperate with Him.

A farmer knows that if he wants 15 acres of produce, he'd better sow 15 acres of seed. He can't just throw out a few leftover handfuls of seed, eat the rest, and then expect to reap a bountiful harvest.

This is where it gets convicting. Too many people in God's family want a big payday from heaven even when they sow very little or nothing at all. Rather than honoring God with the first and best of their resources, they consume it. A farmer isn't fooling anyone but himself if he sows sparingly but thinks he's in for a bountiful harvest. The same is true for any believer—that's why Galatians 6:7 says we can't fool God.

4. Your harvest depends on *where* you sow. When I preached this message at our church, I sprinkled watermelon seeds on the carpet. I told the people that I wanted watermelons, so I was sowing what I wanted to reap. Of course, everyone laughed because I was violating a fundamental rule of sowing. I was "planting" my watermelon seeds in an environment that was not conducive to their growth. In biblical terms, I was planting good seed in bad soil.

You can't plant your seed just anywhere—you have to plant it in soil that is designed to receive and nourish the seed. In the spiritual realm, we sow in good soil by investing in that which will allow us to legitimately give thanks to God. Paul explained it this way in our text:

> Now He who supplies seed to the sower and bread for
> food will supply and multiply your seed for sowing and
> increase the harvest of your righteousness; you will be
> enriched in everything for all liberality, which through us
> is producing *thanksgiving to God* (2 Corinthians 9:10-11).

So the question is, can you give thanks to God for where you are sowing your seed? Are you sowing it in a place where it will reap a harvest of righteousness that brings praise and glory and thanksgiving to God? If I cannot give thanks to God for where I am sowing my seed, then I ought not to be sowing it there. Giving produces a harvest of righteousness when it benefits others and results in thanksgiving to God.

You don't sow your seeds today and go
out tomorrow looking for the harvest.

5. Your harvest depends on *when* you sow. Galatians 6:9 says we will reap in due time if we don't grow weary. That means you don't sow your seeds today and go out tomorrow looking for the harvest. It takes time for seeds to germinate, plants to grow, and fruit to ripen—unless God overrides this process through a miracle. But remember, miracles are not God's normal way of operating. First there's a sowing season, then a "not growing weary" season, and finally a harvest season.

So don't get frustrated if what you are sowing for Jesus today doesn't come to harvest tomorrow. The key thing to remember is that God is always at work—even during the season between planting and reaping. Sometimes we just can't see what's happening underneath the soil. So be patient for your season of reaping, knowing that even when God is silent, He is not still. God is after your long-term benefit and not just your short-term pleasure.

6. Your harvest depends on *why* you sow. The reason God wants to bless your sowing is to "increase the harvest of your righteousness" (2 Corinthians 9:10). God is interested in meeting your need as long as that will help you grow more like Christ. God isn't nearly as interested in simply increasing your stuff. A lot of people want to be blessed for the blessing's sake. Instead, our desire should be to have a closer walk with God and to share our blessing with others.

//

God can make all grace abound to you. But He wants
to make sure that His grace makes you a better you.

\\

In other words, God is not interested in blessing you with a new car so you can be a carnal driver behind the wheel. He's not interested in giving you a bigger house so you can be more unrighteous in it. God is not interested in just the external. He says, "I want to increase the righteousness of your inner person. I want to draw you closer to Myself; I want you to follow Me more obediently." Yes, God can make all grace abound to you. But He wants to make sure that His grace makes you a better you.

One last thing. Notice that Paul said in 2 Corinthians 9:10 that God is the one who supplies seed to the sower. Even the seed you sow comes from God. It's all of grace. God has this thing so covered that once He sees a need, He provides you with seed that will eventually produce a harvest of blessing. And when the need is met, He also supplies more seed for replanting so there can be a further harvest and then additional seed for even the harvest beyond that.

God has given you everything you need in order to carry out His commandments and principles in your relationships with others. But it is up to you to obey Him by doing whatever He asks you to do. Sowing involves investing your time, talents, treasures, and energy in the lives of those around you. God's law says that as you do that— reflecting Him as a horizontal Jesus to others—He will then multiply your seed and return to you a harvest.

3

ENCOURAGING
ONE ANOTHER

On October 24, 1929, our nation faced one of the darkest and most devastating dates in its history. On this day, the stock market crashed, hurling individuals, families, and ultimately our entire society into the menacing grip of the Great Depression. When the Great Depression hit, lives were turned upside down. Businesses went belly-up. Employment opportunities vanished in the economic collapse. Suicide claimed far too many.

Most people found a way to get by. But the cumulative psychological, physiological, spiritual, financial, and emotional impact of that season left its scars. It changed people in the very core of their being. Some folks felt as if they lost more than their money—they lost themselves.

Fast-forward to today, and you may see something similar in the lives of many of those around you. America emerged from the Great Depression and from recessions that followed, yet many people remain smothered under layers of disappointment. This grim reality blankets believers and unbelievers alike. The weight of it hangs heavy in the air, altering dreams, destroying hope, and spreading fear, disillusionment, and despair.

As a pastor, I have heard many of the stories firsthand. I have seen the look on a woman's face when she is past giving up. I have heard the emptiness in a couple's conversation when they no longer believe what they have is worth fighting for. I can recognize the vacant stare before the first word is even spoken. The sparkle is gone, the light has dimmed, and that which makes us most human—love—is like a carrot on a stick, close enough to tempt but too far off to truly embrace.

These stories share one overarching theme: Life has simply not been fair.

The difficulties may vary—strained relationships, family dysfunctions, addictive vices, dead-end jobs, financial hardship, spiritual dryness, emotional struggles—but the results are often the same. The symptoms include cynicism, boredom, detachment, anger, obsession, anxiety, distraction, and gloom.

> Too many of us face our own great
> depressions on a regular basis.

Some choose to cope by staying in bed and pulling the covers up over their eyes. Others turn to pills and medication to fix what is broken inside. Many lose themselves in entertainment, run to illicit relationships or porn, or turn to alcohol to take the sting out of their open wound of discontent. Whether through escapism or indulgence, these people are trying to find a way to deal with their agony. The Great Depression was a one-time event, but too many of us face our own great depressions on a regular basis.

We All Struggle Somehow

This malady is all too common in our lives, homes, and churches. If you suffer from depression, you are not alone. Neither you nor those around you who experience the same struggle are to be judged, discounted, or belittled. Such is life for far too many, oftentimes through no fault of their own. It is the result of living as sinful beings in a fallen world.

This isn't unique to contemporary Western life. The Bible is full of men and women who faced discouragement at a deep level. King David was often either up or deeply down, asking himself why his soul despaired within him (Psalms 42:5,11; 43:5). King Solomon, a man of great wisdom and clarity, wrote, "The day of one's death is better than the day of one's birth" (Ecclesiastes 7:1). After Elijah's victory on Mount Carmel, he plunged to such depths that he asked that he might die (1 Kings 19:4). Jonah asked God to kill him because he was so despondent (Jonah 4:3,8). Jeremiah is known as the weeping prophet. Even the great apostle Paul said, "For we do not want you to be unaware, brethren, of our affliction which came to us in Asia, that we were burdened excessively, beyond our strength, so that we despaired even of life" (2 Corinthians 1:8).

Life may serve some great things on your plate. We have many things to experience and enjoy. But you will sample the bitter taste of hardships, emptiness, and brokenness at some point. I'm speaking from experience—I'm no stranger to bitter tastes myself. These feelings of despondency used to visit me regularly and still do from time to time. They could be a part of what I do because they would often come at the same time each week—just following the mountaintop of proclamation.

Without a doubt, five a.m. on Sunday mornings is the highlight of my week. I literally hop out of bed ready for the day. I've prepared the message, my heart is filled with what I want to communicate, I've prayed for the hearers, and I'm ready to see what God will do. I head to church to participate in two back-to-back services lasting nearly two hours each. My teaching time lasts from 45 minutes to an hour, and when I preach, I leave it all on the field. I invest my emotions, strength, mind, and spirit. Preaching is the passion of my soul.

Seemingly without fail, though, just a few hours after it's over, I slide from the mountaintop into a valley. Exhaustion seeps in, the blue sky turns a bit grayer, my enthusiasm wanes, and I quickly find my easy chair. It's a cycle I've learned to accept. I wait it out and trust that it, too, will pass.

In those times, I get a firsthand taste of what so many people feel and experience every day. I believe this has developed in me an authentic compassion for those who struggle with discouragement. It isn't something you can just tell someone to set aside. You can't just expect people to be happy, move on, and enjoy life. Oftentimes, what they are experiencing goes beyond just the emotional—it is a combination of the social, physiological, and more.

From Cloud Cover to New Covenant

Far too many people today live underneath this constant cloud cover and fog. When something good happens, the sun peeks through with a moment of brilliance, only to disappear as fast as it came.

But just as the government of the United States under the leadership of Franklin Delano Roosevelt provided a New Deal to lift our country out of the Great Depression, our Father in heaven has provided a new covenant to lift us out of our own despair. The new covenant is God's new deal, giving us what we need to persevere until our situation changes. The new covenant covers us, comforts us, and gives us what we need during our times of discouragement.

Friend, I can't tell you when your situation will change, but God's

Word shows us how to make it until it does. In the book of Hebrews, God reveals how to think when you are experiencing down times and how to treat others who are experiencing discouragement as well. Remember, this Christian life isn't just about you. God has placed you in a context of community on purpose. He has put us in connection with each other so we can have a hand in each other's well-being.

Encourage One Another

The author of Hebrews exhorts us, "Encourage one another day after day" (Hebrews 3:13). We also read, "Let us consider how to stimulate one another to love and good deeds, not forsaking our own assembling together, as is the habit of some, but encouraging one another; and all the more as you see the day drawing near" (Hebrews 10:24-25).

God wants each of us in the body of Christ to be a vessel through which He can strengthen other believers. And He wants other believers to strengthen you. This is the life-on-life impact we are to lean into with each other. This is how we can fully live out and embrace the maximum potential of who God created us to be.

As you learn to identify with others in their pain and encourage them in the hard times, you become the hands and feet of Jesus Christ to those around you. You become a horizontal Jesus to others, encouraging them with His hope, love, kindness, and grace.

On the days when you don't need encouragement for yourself, keep in mind that one reason you are placed in the body of Christ is to give that encouragement to others. Do it, because your day is coming. Disappointments have a way of showing up when you least expect them. They sneak up on all of us, so everyone needs some encouragement now and then.

*If you don't need encouragement right now, now is
the time to be that encouragement to someone else.*

How can you position yourself to receive that encouragement when you need it? It's simple—make sure to be an encourager to others when they need it. Always remember the "it" principle of Luke 6:38—"Give, and *it* will be given to you." The "it" you give away is the "it" you can be confident you will receive.

Will you need encouragement someday? Yes. Will you need to be pointed in the right direction sometime? Yes. Will you need a reminder to hang in there because things are going to get better? Yes. So remember—even if you don't need encouragement right now, now is the time to *be* that encouragement to someone else.

The book of Hebrews was written to Jewish Christians who were considering throwing in the towel. They wanted to quit. Some of these people were thinking, "I can't take this anymore—following Jesus is too hard. We're losing friends. We're losing property. Some of us have even gone to jail." These individuals were tempted to look back, remembering what their lives were like before they were persecuted for the name of Christ.

Just who authored Hebrews is not certain, but his message is crystal clear. He repeatedly encourages his readers with promises of hope and exhortations to persevere. He knows these believers feel like quitting and returning to their old lifestyle, but he wrote this book to say, "Keep going. Don't stop. Don't turn around. Don't go backward."

We need to hear the message of Hebrews today. Its truths and principles show us how to relate to one another when disappointments come. It warns us of the temptations that often accompany our struggles. And it provides the perspective we need to overcome.

The New Deal

To encourage his readers that following after Jesus Christ is worth every effort, the writer of Hebrews highlights the new agreement and new covering. He says, "This is the covenant that I will make with them after those days, says the Lord: I will put My laws upon their heart, and on their mind I will write them" (10:16). The writer refers to the covenant—God's agreement with His people that describes how we are to live with Him and the blessings He provides.

Those of us who come underneath the covering of this covenant by trusting in Jesus Christ as our Savior are reminded that even though we may be struggling and going through a rough time, we have something to look forward to. There is a plan in place, a new deal of sorts, assuring us of covering, protection, provision, and more if we will just hang in there and keep moving forward.

> Therefore, brethren, since we have confidence to enter the holy place by the blood of Jesus, by a new and living way which He inaugurated for us through the veil, that is, His flesh, and since we have a great priest over the house of God, let us draw near with a sincere heart in full assurance of faith, having our hearts sprinkled clean from an evil conscience and our bodies washed with pure water. Let us hold fast the confession of our hope without wavering, for He who promised is faithful (10:19-23).

Instead of turning around and running away from the faith, we are encouraged to "draw near." Instead of letting issues and disappointments create in us a spirit of fear and doubt, we are to live with "full assurance" and "hold fast the confession of our hope." As we read, "He who promised is faithful."

Drawing near to God is different from religious ritual. It is a bold approach to His throne of grace and mercy. Holding fast the confession of our hope means being real with God in His presence—ready to access the benefits of the covenant He has in store for each one of us.

These truths are so critical to living out a fruitful and abundant Christian life, and yet we often forget them. And when we do remember, we often neglect to remind each other of them. Have you ever noticed how easy it is to have faith when things seem to be going your way? Or how easy it is to communicate with God when all is well? Yet when hardship comes, the report from the doctor wasn't as planned, the finances get hit, the relationship sours...that's when we need all the more to draw near to God. Yet it is also in those times that we forget to do just that.

Knowing this, God built into His body a way to remind each of us what we are to do when those times come. He did this by planting His compassion and love in each of our hearts and giving us a directive to encourage one another. When you no longer feel like drawing near, that's the most important time for you to draw near. When you don't feel like making contact with heaven, that's when you need to make contact with heaven. We all need to be reminded of this reality when we are in the midst of forgetting it.

We have been put here *on* purpose, *for* a purpose—
to reflect His glory and His image to those around us.

Life is relational. Life is connection. Yet in our fast-paced schedules, we often feel as if the only relational connections we have outside our homes are at work or in Sunday school or small groups. And while these places and things are nice, God doesn't want us to limit our interactions to these places. He wants to remind us that we have been put here *on* purpose, *for* a purpose—to reflect His glory and His image to those around us. One way we do this is by encouraging one another to keep our eyes, hearts, minds, and hope set on Him because the payoff for so doing will be worth it in the end.

When you go through struggles, you need someone to come alongside you and remind you that there is hope ahead. You need to hear a word to point your thoughts in the direction of God and His goodness again. So do I. We all do. That is why we should always be mindful of the great gift we provide as we encourage others when they need it the most.

Gaps Before the Promises

So many believers in Jesus Christ don't see God's promises fulfilled in their lives because they shrink back in difficult times rather than drawing near in faith. We have just seen that "He who promised is faithful." This is a common theme throughout Scripture.

But there is another pattern in Scripture (and in our lives) that we often forget. After God delivers His promises, we usually experience a gap before we see their fulfillment. A gap is the period of time between the promise and its fulfillment. God uses this time to prepare us to receive His blessing.

For example, God's promise that Abraham would receive his son Isaac came a full 25 years before Isaac was born. During those 25 years, God was preparing Abraham to receive the fulfillment of the promise—developing Abraham's character and building his faith. Gaps like this are frequent in our lives as God sets us on the path to His provision. But instead of cooperating with God and drawing near to Him, many of us choose to draw back. It's easy to just give up and assume that we misunderstood the promise. Or we rationalize away God's covenantal covering over our lives and simply lose the motivation to hang in there, do good, and seek God each day.

In times like these, we need each other all the more. Just as a toddler needs a mother to continually encourage her to keep trying to walk even though she falls down again and again, we need each other in the body of Christ to encourage us. We need reminders that we will one day reach the promises if we don't sit down and give up. This is why we are to "consider how to stimulate one another to love and good deeds, not forsaking our own assembling together, as is the habit of some, but *encouraging one another*; and all the more as you see the day drawing near" (Hebrews 10:24-25).

A Church of Cheerleaders

One of the main reasons you are to come to church and to participate in a small group of some sort is so others can stimulate you and you can do the same for them. Your fellow believers are to be encouraging you and motivating you to do good works, and you likewise are to do the same for them. Just think how a good cup of coffee perks you up in the morning. That's how we are to be to each other—energizing one another to hang in there, to keep going when times seem tough, and to do good things for God's kingdom.

When my son played football for Baylor, the team was not known for winning. In fact, they were known for losing most of their games during that time. Yet every time I went to see one of their games, the cheerleaders were on the sidelines, cheering on the Baylor Bears. This is because the cheerleaders' role is to support their team regardless of how things are going on the field. Similarly, we are to be cheerleaders for one another in the body of Christ. Even on your worst day, someone will come alongside you and cheer you on to keep having faith, keep trusting God, and keep pursuing His agenda in your life. And when you have come through that difficult time, you can become that cheerleader for someone else as well.

That doesn't mean we always agree with the decisions other people make, just as cheerleaders and fans don't always agree with the plays the coach calls. But we can cheer for a change in momentum, a reversal in the score, and a better performance moving forward. The word translated "encourage" in Hebrews 10:25 means to come alongside to help, strengthen, or support. When would someone need another to come alongside to help, strengthen, or support? When they are down, when they are discouraged, or when things are not flowing well in their lives. That is the critical time when we need to be there for one another. And when we are the ones who are discouraged, when things are not flowing in our own lives, that's when we need others to be there for us.

A church is a network of believers who encourage each other to keep going even when they feel like quitting. Only by drawing near to the Lord will we discover the ultimate purpose God has in store for us. In the church where I pastor, some single people are discouraged and tired of waiting for a mate. Some career-minded individuals are tired of waiting for a breakthrough at work. Some families are feeling the strain of life and its demands, and they are tired of just trying to make it. Name any challenge, and you can probably find people who need to be encouraged to keep going until God brings about a change.

The best way to encourage someone with the truth is by sharing an appropriate passage of Scripture.

In situations like these, we need to encourage one another in a spirit of love and truth (Ephesians 4:15; Titus 1:9). The best way to encourage someone with the truth is by sharing an appropriate passage of Scripture. Paul tells us in Romans, "For whatever was written in earlier times was written for our instruction, so that through perseverance and the encouragement of the Scriptures we might have hope" (Romans 15:4).

Just as an excellent cheerleader at a football game is prepared and isn't just making stuff up along the way, excellent encouragers in the church are familiar with the truth of God's Word and can apply it to other people's lives. They can bring hope through the "encouragement of the Scriptures." That is our greatest means for bringing lasting encouragement to others.

The right word spoken at the right time can change someone's trajectory or even revive their life. Offering encouragement is like watering the soil around a drooping plant to bring it to life again. That's why it's essential that we stay connected in the church, in small groups, and in serving ministries—so we can be there for each other. We are to encourage one another all the more as the day of Christ's returning draws near.

The apostle Paul writes, "Therefore encourage one another and build up one another, just as you also are doing" (1 Thessalonians 5:11). You and I build up people through our encouragement. We make them stronger. They make us stronger. Building up people requires skill and intention, just as building a house does. We are to use encouragement to keep other believers moving forward spiritually in their Christian life and not drifting backward (Hebrews 3:12-13.)

Let your words and actions be seasoned with encouragement so others are stronger after being with you.

4

LOVING ONE ANOTHER

Designers and product manufacturers are known by their brands. A swoosh on a garment stands for more than a company. It stands for a purpose, a look, a feel...an attitude. An apple with a bite taken out of it alerts consumers to a certain standard of quality, functionality, and creativity. Golden arches mean much more than simply an "M"—they shout convenience, efficiency, economy, taste, and sometimes a place for young children to play.

Trademarks, logos, and other branding tools distinguish a company, product, or service. They make something unique and set it apart from anything else. Branding sets the stage for consumers' expectations. It communicates much more than a name and a function—it also communicates values, atmosphere, and intention. It creates an identity and connects it to a larger and highly desirable context.

After all, how things connect is key on many levels. When we consider a potential purchase, we often want to know how it will help us do what we do and connect with others. In fact, we often choose products or services that bring us closer together with one another.

For example, why are such games as Fantasy Football successful?

It's not just about winning or racking up points, although those are enjoyable. It has more to do with the way these games connect people who share a common goal. People exchange texts on game days to brag or to bash, to check other competitors' picks, or just to discuss strategy. Strip all of that away, and the game probably wouldn't have consumed our nation as it has.

People thrive on community. We need each other. Whether for companionship, encouragement, or just plain fun, we enjoy doing things together. In fact, we were created for relationship. That's what makes God's "brand" all the more important. Yes, God has a brand as well. His identity, logo, and values set Him and His people apart from all others. As members of the body of Christ, we are to manifest His brand in what we say and do so that there is no question who we are and who we represent.

What is God's brand? It isn't people carrying Bibles underneath their arms. Neither is it Christianese—language designed to make some people sound holier or more spiritual than others. It isn't church attendance on Sundays or Wednesdays. No, God's brand is not an external look or activity. Instead, it's ingrained in the very fabric of life.

To know God's brand is to know His heart and His character. To reflect His brand is to reflect Christ Himself. Jesus told us what God's brand is—the one trait we are to be known for—when He gathered His disciples together in the upper room to give them His final message prior to His death and resurrection. In that room, He told them the identifying factor of belonging to Him as His follower.

Jesus summarizes the brand in John 13:31-32, where we find the word "glorify" (or "glorified") five times.

> When [Judas] had gone out, Jesus said, "Now is the Son
> of Man glorified, and God is glorified in Him; if God is

glorified in Him, God will also glorify Him in Himself, and will glorify Him immediately."

As you know, to glorify something is to advertise it or show if off. It means to put it on display. In these two verses, Jesus shows us that the Son glorifies the Father and the Father glorifies the Son. In essence, they advertise each other, like billboards reflecting each other's goodness.

> We are to live in a way that glorifies the Father and the Son—to reflect His brand.

As Jesus continues His discourse with His friends and followers, we discover that we too are called to put this glory on display. It's as if we were God's own advertising agency! Jesus tells us that we are to live in a way that glorifies the Father and the Son—to reflect His brand.

> Little children, I am with you a little while longer. You will seek Me; and as I said to the Jews, now I also say to you, "Where I am going, you cannot come." A new commandment I give to you, that you *love one another*, even as I have loved you, that you also *love one another*. By this all men will know that you are My disciples, if you have *love for one another* (verses 33-35).

Three times in this passage Jesus tells us we are to love others. Three times He takes us to this all-important principle—His brand. In fact, He comes right out and says that if we love one another, all men will know that we are reflecting Him as His disciples. So the question we need to answer today is, what is love? How do we love one another?

Unfortunately, the word "love" has fallen on some hard times as of late. It can be used for so many things that it has lost some of the potency of its original meaning. People might say, "I love chocolate cake" or "I love this team." "Love" has become a catchall word lacking the full impact of its original meaning. It doesn't always carry the depth it once did.

It's like the letter a woman wrote to her former boyfriend, whom she had just broken up with a month earlier. "Dearest Ricky, I just want to write to tell you how much I miss you. I want to tell you that I still love you, and I can't get you off of my mind. I really, really love you." The woman then signed the letter and added, "P.S. Congratulations on winning the lottery."

As you can see, that wasn't really love at all.

When someone can give you something you want, you may be motivated to connect with them. But that's not God's definition of love.

To love is to prioritize someone else's needs above your own.

When the Bible uses the Greek word for this kind of love (*agape*), it's talking about a *compassionate and righteous pursuit of another person's well-being*. To love is to prioritize someone else's needs above your own. It doesn't equate to liking someone. In fact, you can love people you don't even like because love is an intentional choice to do what is best for them.

Truth be told, you may recall times when you did not "like" your boss, your child, or your mate. The emotional connection just wasn't there. Disagreements or poor choices had accumulated and taken their toll. Yet you continued to love them because love is an action, a commitment, a choice to do what's best for the other person.

We can't always control our feelings, but we can control our actions. Jesus distinguishes love from an emotional feeling when He actually *commands* us to love—"A new commandment I give to you." We can rarely command our feelings to do anything at all, but we can command our actions. We can use our mind and our will to make commitments that guide our choices.

Think about it. When you have warm, mushy feelings for someone (the popular understanding of love), you don't have to be commanded to do anything at all for him or her. You'll do whatever you're asked—and much more! But Jesus presents His call to love as a command. That is our first clue that the love Jesus is talking about is not the hearts-and-flowers love we celebrate every February. It's much more than that.

Biblical love is a choice to do good for another person regardless of what we feel. It is a decision to compassionately and righteously pursue the betterment of another person. This is why you can even love your enemies according to Christ's command.

Learning to Love like Jesus

If you come down with a cold, you will have telltale symptoms. If you come down with the flu, you will have other symptoms—an upset stomach, achiness, and perhaps a cough. In other words, your external condition reveals that something is not right internally. Likewise, as a serious follower of Jesus Christ, you will manifest a "symptom"—your love for others. The external evidence (love) shows that you are Christ's disciple. Others can get a glimpse into your internal, vertical relationship with God by noticing your external, horizontal relationship with others. This is because disciples of Jesus are visual, verbal followers, not simply church members, religious people, or folks who read the Bible.

God has plenty of fans but very few disciples.

One of the problems God faces in His body today is that He's got plenty of fans but very few disciples. He's got a fairly large fan club—people who will show up to applaud Him on Sunday—but bear in mind, that is not the definition Jesus Christ gave of a disciple. Jesus said, "By this all men will know that you are My disciples, *if you have love for one another.*" Jesus ties our discipleship to the action of love. That is the external manifestation of the internal commitment to discipleship.

Again, love does not primarily have to do with feelings, although it can include them. Rather, it is based on your commitment to follow Jesus Christ. That is why and how you can love people whom you might struggle to like.

Have you ever wondered why God may have put difficult people in your life? These are people whom you find it challenging to get along with, let alone love. They say things that get on your nerves, or they do things that constantly put you on guard. Or there is simply a personality rift that isn't even directly tied to any one thing. These people are in our lives for a reason—God uses them to teach us how to love as He did. The apostle Paul writes, "God demonstrates His own love toward us, in that while we were yet sinners, Christ died for us" (Romans 5:8).

God acted out His love for us when we were unlovable. When we were annoying, irregular, unlikeable, unpredictable...even then, God demonstrated His love for us in giving up the greatest sacrifice, His Son Jesus Christ, on our behalf. That is the truest revelation of love—doing something on someone's behalf that they cannot do for themselves, especially when they don't appreciate what you've done. Because God has modeled perfect love for us, we can imitate Him and reflect His love for others.

Teenagers in the Family of God

If you have a teenage child, you know that technology has created a new kind of teenager. Teens have so many online options for connecting with their friends, entertainment, and so on, they can live in their rooms and never come out except to eat. They can access their whole world right there in one room, so the only time you see them is when they wander into the kitchen to see what you have in the refrigerator. And you can be sure they'll let you know if the refrigerator is empty.

In other words, today's teens could actually develop a habit of coming out to be fed rather than to be family. If that happened, they would want you to give them something, but they wouldn't want to connect to life at home by giving something themselves.

///

Our experience of God's love for us is
directly tied to our love for others.

\\\\\\\\\\\\\\\\\\\\\\\\\\\\\\\\\\\\

Friend, God has some teenagers like that in His family as well. In fact, many of those who make up the body of Christ are still teenagers.

They go to church each Sunday to be fed. They look in the refrigerator of worship to see what songs are going to be sung to them. They enjoy the benefits of the ministries that serve them, but when they are asked to love someone, support someone, stand with someone, listen to someone, or help out someone, they are nowhere to be found. By that, they are saying, "I'm not going to love anyone but myself."

The problem is, our experience of God's love for us is directly tied to our love for others. By choosing to serve yourself rather than others, you are actually short-circuiting the manifestation and results of God's love for you. You are actually limiting yourself by failing to love others.

I don't know about your family, but when my kids rejected one of their siblings or didn't respond when a brother or sister needed help, that affected my relationship with them. It changed our conversations—we now had to talk about why they thought they didn't need to help out their sibling. It also changed what I gave them—I sometimes had to withhold good things so they gained wisdom by experiencing the consequences of their actions.

What you do for others affects what God does for you.

As we are learning, what you do for others affects what God does for you. This is true in our homes, churches, and work environments. When people are team players and serve those around them, they can receive more. My kids knew that people in our family couldn't say, "I love you, Mom and Dad, but I don't really care about your other kids. Feed me, but if they don't eat, that's fine. Just make sure there is enough for me." No, they knew that things just didn't roll that way in the Evans home.

Well, friend, things don't roll that way in God's family either.

Remember, in God's family there is no such thing as an only child. When Jesus taught us the Lord's Prayer, He instructed us to pray, "*Our* Father who is in heaven..." He didn't teach us to say, "My Daddy, who is in heaven..." This is a family. We all have one Father, and He holds us accountable to love our siblings. It's a command, not a suggestion.

God wants every believer to become a functional part of a local church body and not just a visiting part. He wants everyone to contribute to the greater needs of the family. He wants others to look into this family from the outside and see what the members do for each other—and be attracted to come on in. Have you ever experienced the joy of a close-knit family, where the members are really into each other and help each other out from a heart of true care and love? These families are rare, but when they exist, others will often look in and wish that they had a family like that. A family is attractive and appealing when its members truly love each other and care for each other's emotions and needs.

Our Lord wants this happening in the family of God—people loving each other in ways that are so dynamic, real, and rich that others see what is happening and glorify God. They are drawn not only to the people but also to God Himself. This doesn't happen because everyone is perfect or because everyone always likes everyone else. It happens because committed, compassionate love is so appealing. It's what we were created for.

///

Satan doesn't want us to be effective at
advertising the glory of God or manifesting
His brand of love to those around us.

\\

This is one of the main reasons why the enemy seeks to divide the body of Christ. Division, quarrels, and the like are opposites of Christ's command to love. Where people are divisive, selfish, and quick to run away, God is not being glorified. Satan doesn't want us to be effective at advertising the glory of God or manifesting His brand of love to those around us, so he looks for ways to build walls between us. He'll use racial prejudice, personality differences, class distinctions...anything to keep us apart. Satan is always on the prowl, looking for opportunities to disrupt the body of Christ and destroy our unity. If he can accomplish that, he makes our brand ineffective. This is also why Paul instructs us to identify and instruct those who cause division in the church (Romans 16:17).

The Light of Love

The apostle John sometimes refers to himself as "the apostle whom Jesus loved." It's appropriate, then, for us to take a look at what John had to say about this important topic and why we should be so proactive about loving.

> The one who says he is in the Light and yet hates his brother is in the darkness until now. The one who loves his brother abides in the Light and there is no cause for stumbling in him. But the one who hates his brother is in the darkness and walks in the darkness, and does not know where he is going because the darkness has blinded his eyes (1 John 2:9-11).

This passage clearly shows that if you are a believer who doesn't love others—who is not meaningfully invested in the life of God's family—then you're walking in darkness. When you're in the dark, you can't see where you're going. And when you can't see where you're going, you're likely to stumble. Many believers are not seeing where

God is taking them simply because they aren't living out this command to love others.

When God tells you to love and you say no, He allows you to operate outside of His divine light and guidance. You get to live your life apart from His illumination and wisdom. You can't see His light showing you where you ought to go, what you ought to do, and with whom.

You can see clearly only when there is light.

Your horizontal relationships with others directly affect your vertical relationship with God. If you are looking to God only for yourself—so He will feed you, clothe you, guide you, and love you—your experience of God will suffer. If you aren't willing to be used by God to help someone else in a meaningful way, you cannot expect to experience everything God has for you. When you willingly choose to live in the dark, you lose the full benefit of God's light in your life. That's just the way it works. To choose not to love is to cast off any possibility of intimacy with God (1 John 4:8,12).

Many people come to me complaining that their lives are cloudy and foggy. Things just aren't making sense for them. When people tell me this, one of the first things I do is check their horizontal relationships. If your horizontal relationships with others are hindering the work God wants to do in your vertical relationship with Him, that needs to be the primary focus of attention.

Love in Deed and Truth

The apostle John continues to connect our horizontal and vertical relationships. In 1 John 3:17-18 we read, "Whoever has the world's goods, and sees his brother in need and closes his heart against him, how does the love of God abide in him? Little children, let us not love with word or with tongue, but in deed and truth."

In this passage, John describes love as a tangible act of facilitating the well-being of others. It is coming alongside them in physical, tangible ways in order to help meet legitimate needs. It is doing and saying things that promote life in them. John comes right out and says that if you can't share life with others through actions or words of love, God's love does not abide in you. Conversely, if God's love abides in you, you will help others simply because God's love in you will overflow through you.

///

Give someone else more of you, and
you will experience more of God.

\\\

Not only that, but whatever you give horizontally, that's what you can expect vertically. If you do not have love for others, you're not likely to sense the fullness of God's love in you.

Do you want a greater sense of God's love? Do you want to experience more of God's presence? Do you want to embrace more of God's reality? Then follow this exhortation from John, the beloved: If you give love to someone else, God's love will likewise abide in you. Give someone else more of you, and you will experience more of God.

Keep in mind that you're not getting more of God. If you've trusted in Jesus Christ for your salvation, you already have all of God you will ever have. All of God is available to you. That's why John used the word "abide," which has to do with the experience of God. It has to do with how much of God you can experience. As you tangibly love others, you open the door for God to give you more of an abiding sense of His presence and His love.

John presses this principle even further. "Beloved, let us love one another, for love is from God; and everyone who loves is born of God and knows God. The one who does not love does not know God, for God is love" (1 John 4:7-8). To "not know God," in this passage refers to your experience of God. Scripture makes it clear here and in other places that your love for others horizontally has a direct effect on your experience of God's love for you. Again, it does not impact how much God loves you, for His love is perfect and complete, but it does affect how much of that perfect and complete love you get to experience and see manifested in your life.

This important truth is often overlooked. John goes on to emphasize it even more when he says, "In this is love, not that we loved God, but that He loved us and sent His Son to be the propitiation for our sins. Beloved, if God so loved us, we also ought to love one another" (verses 10-11).

///

When you are loving, you are *doing* what He *is*.

\\\

John emphasizes in this passage that God's love for us was sacrificial. It came at a time when we weren't looking for Him. This came about, as we saw earlier in verse 8, because "God is love." Love is the very nature of who God is, and He defines Himself by that attribute. So when you are loving others the way the Bible describes God's love, you are connected to God in a uniquely powerful way simply because you are tying in directly to who He is. You are *doing* what He *is*, so He is involved in what you are doing at a new level. You are opening the floodgates of His presence and power in your life.

John continues to remind us that love is God's dominating character quality. "We have come to know and have believed the love which God has for us. God is love, and the one who abides in love abides in God, and God abides in him" (verse 16). John makes it clear that when you hang out in love (sharing loving actions and words), you are actually hanging out with God. How much of God do you want to experience? That's how much you ought to be tangibly loving others.

No Fear in Love

So why would we ever shy away from loving others? One reason has to do with fear. Maybe we think they will take advantage of us. Maybe we feel that they will be ungrateful. Maybe we think we will have to sacrifice too much of what we want or what we need in order to teach that class, join that ministry, listen to that person's problem, or help that neighbor. But the good thing about loving the way the Bible says to love is that "there is no fear in love; but perfect love casts out fear" (verse 18).

You can never outlove God.

You can never outlove God. Sure, you may love someone through a tangible act, a listening ear, or any number of ways, and that love might not ever be reciprocated. But God took note. God saw it. God noticed it, and He will respond to it. His abiding love will meet your needs.

If you are living in fear, you are not living in love. If you are trying to protect yourself by not fully loving, then you don't understand God's command. Biblical love casts out fear. What is the opposite of fear? Peace. God's love produces peace.

Peace is a pricey commodity in today's world. People try to buy it through any number of ventures, distractions, pills, relationships, and more. But God says it is yours, free of charge, if you will love others in His name.

More than that, He says He will answer your prayers when you love. In 1 John 3:21-22, we read, "Beloved, if our heart does not condemn us, we have confidence before God; and whatever we ask we receive from Him, because we keep His commandments and do the things that are pleasing in His sight."

God will literally give you something back when He sees you loving others. And again, I'm not just talking about having loving feelings for others. When God sees you compassionately and righteously pursuing the well-being of others (whether you like them or not), His payoff is pretty steep. He says He will answer more of your prayers.

Loving others gets you peace from God, and loving others gets your prayers answered.

Could it be that your prayers aren't being answered because you aren't sharing your love? Could it be you're asking God for what you want from Him, but you're not sharing with others the things He wants to give them through you? Loving others gets you peace from God, and loving others gets your prayers answered. In fact, you are told you can now come before God with confidence that whatever you ask you will receive. That's the power of love.

"Love one another" is not just any old commandment. It is the greatest commandment (after loving God), and it carries the greatest benefits—experiencing God's presence, His love, His peace, and His power in your life.

Real, authentic love has a way of
editing out our mistakes.

One of the greatest benefits of demonstrating love to others is found in 1 Peter 4:8, where we read that "love covers a multitude of sins." When our son Jonathan played football in college, his coaches made what is called a "highlight reel" for him to give to NFL scouts. The highlight reel showed all of his great plays. It didn't show his mistakes. Of course, the scouts had access to the full reel, and they knew Jonathan had messed up on some plays, but that's not what they got when they received the highlight reel.

Love is like the editing software of your life's highlight reel. When you stand before God at the judgment seat of Christ, all your thoughts and actions will be revealed. God will examine them to determine the rewards you will receive in heaven. However, 1 Peter 4:8 tells us that love will cover a multitude of sins. Real, authentic love has a way of editing out our mistakes. Now, if *that* isn't a reason to truly love others, I don't know what is!

I'll never forget an experience I had at Alexander Hamilton Elementary School, just three blocks from where I was raised in Baltimore. I must have been in the fifth or sixth grade at the time. I tagged along with the custodian to the boiler room, and he began to show me around. In the middle of the boiler room was an enormous tank that held all the hot water that was piped to radiators throughout the building. That's how the rooms were heated.

On the side of the big tank, I saw a little tube with some water in it. When I noticed the tube, I asked the janitor why it was there. He replied, "Anthony, this tank holds gallons and gallons and gallons of water, but we can't go into the tank to see how much is in there. It's just too hot. So instead, we look at the tube, and it tells us. The tube is small, but it's accurate. By looking at the water level in the tube, we can determine the water level in the tank."

I can't see how much of God's presence you are experiencing in your life. You can't see that in me either. But, friend, there is a tube. And that tube is the indicator to let you know on the outside how much God is working in me on the inside. That tube is love.

If we can't love each other, care for each other, pray for each other, walk with each other...then that tube is telling us we're not experiencing as much of God as we could be. We can sing our hearts out in church or raise our hands to Him all we want, but if the tube is empty, we're just making a lot of noise. Without love, there is no true manifestation of God in our lives.

Love makes the world go round because God is love, and "in Him all things hold together" (Colossians 1:17). Love is entirely connected to God—that is, the biblical definition of love, not the emotional feelings that come and go. Love others, and you are intimately abiding in the greatest, most powerful Presence in the universe.

In other words, when you love someone and have his or her back, you can count on God to have yours.

5

Connecting with One Another

It may not be a popular notion—that what you do for others affects what God does for you—but a lot of thought, contemplation, and discussion went into how to position this book. What would we call it? What would the subtitle be? Should we really say that the way we interact with others affects the way God interacts with us? Some people felt that might be going too far. After all, isn't God's love unconditional? Isn't His love perfect? We obviously don't control a providential and sovereign God, so should the subtitle and content indicate that what we do can impact what He does? Doesn't that put boundaries on what God can do, as if He were a convenient and predictable "God in a box"?

But in all the discussions and debates, my spirit kept coming back to the Scriptures. And the Scriptures make clear that what we do *can* impact what He does. Of course, God can do whatever He wants, but His normal way of doing things is to take our actions into account.

And since what we do *can* influence what He does, wouldn't you want to know what you can do about that now?

I know I do. I want to experience every bit of God I can. If how I treat others can have an impact on that, then I want to know what to do, and I want to do it. Since you picked up this book and are reading it, I imagine you feel the same way too.

So let me give you some background on how I arrived at positioning this subject as I did. As I studied to preach this series and write this book, I saw that the Bible repeatedly showed a direct correlation between God's interaction with us (our vertical relationship) and our interactions with others (our horizontal relationships). God tells us that forgiving others affects His relational forgiveness of us (Matthew 6:14-15), and we find a similar pattern in several other passages. If God Himself is so bold as to make this reality clear in His Word, I didn't want to shy away from it.

Our role as the body of Christ is to model His life, values, and love—to be like a horizontal Jesus to the people around us. And in so doing, we enrich and deepen our vertical relationship with God and experience more of Him in our lives. It's a win-win scenario. Others benefit as we reflect Jesus to them, and we benefit as we experience God more fully.

Is God's love unconditional? Yes.

Is God's grace free? Yes.

Do we have any effect on our salvation other than believing in Christ alone through faith alone? No.

But is our experience of God's power and presence in our lives at times influenced by our interactions with others and for them? Yes, it is.

You cannot grow closer to God and ignore your brother.

Our vertical relationship with God is intricately connected with our horizontal relationships with one another. You cannot grow closer to God and ignore your brother. God's Word makes that clear, as we saw in 1 John 4:20: "If someone says, 'I love God,' and hates his brother, he is a liar; for the one who does not love his brother whom he has seen, cannot love God whom he has not seen." And if you do not love God, you do not experience the complete manifestation of His abiding presence.

Friend, if you want to experience more of God vertically, you must be dynamically involved with others horizontally. You must be the visible expression of Christ's love to other members of the family of God. The two go together hand in hand. You can't say, "I want to be close to God, but I don't want to deal with His people." When you think, talk, and act like that, you create a breach in the family structure. We don't always emphasize this truth in its practical terms, but we are all members of the body of Christ. We are all parts of God's family, and as family members, we have certain roles and responsibilities.

Your salvation is personal, but it is certainly not private.

The Bible encourages Christians to be active members of a local body of believers because that's the environment where we experience God at a deeper level. That environment involves connectivity—both with God and with others. We all play a part in the family. Your salvation is personal, but it is certainly not private.

The Hunger for Connection

We're living in a day when connection has become a pretty big deal. Now, I'm not computer savvy, but I do know enough to know that the Internet and smartphones have made connecting a priority of everyday life. Computers and tablets and smartphones, Instagram and Pinterest and Twitter...digital media have dominated our connectivity and raised it to another level. All day long, people are communicating with each other through texts, chats, emails, and more. People you know will tag you, and people you don't know hashtag things that interest you. As this happens, our desire for connectivity continues to grow. This is because each of us innately hungers for connection.

We recognize this desire for relationship in our connectivity-crazy culture, but this hunger is not new to twenty-first-century social media. It started with something God had in mind when He created us. This is explained for us in detail in 1 Corinthians 12, which is the most comprehensive statement in the New Testament on the importance of connecting horizontally and vertically. This subject is so critical to the victorious Christian life that the Holy Spirit directed the apostle Paul to commit the entire chapter to the priority of connectivity. The visual image of it can be summarized in verse 27: "Now you are Christ's body, and individually members of it."

When God sets out to give us an illustration of connectivity, He uses something all of us can identify with—a body. Each of us has a physical body, so each of us knows that the body does what the head tells it to do. If the head says, "Walk," the body walks. If the head says, "Raise your arm," the body raises its arm. In other words, our bodies are completely responsive to our brains.

When your brain says one thing and your body does something else, you need to see a doctor. The job of the physical body is to reflect the dictates of the brain.

Scripture is clear that Jesus Christ is the head of the church, which

He calls His body. Therefore, the job of Jesus's body—that's us—is to reflect the dictates of our head, Jesus Christ. To do anything else is dysfunction. To do anything else produces chaos, confusion, and pain. Only when we are properly aligned underneath the goals, visions, and directives of Jesus Christ do we fully function as we were designed.

Members of One Body

In 1 Corinthians 12, the apostle Paul explains the concept of the body of Christ and its members. The word "body" is used 13 times in these verses, often accompanied by the word "member."

When Paul uses the word "body," he is referencing the whole frame. When he speaks about the "members," he is talking about the individual parts that are attached to and comprise the whole frame. We actually get our term "membership" from this concept. The individual members have been created to implement the desires and directives of the brain, Jesus Christ, on behalf of the body.

Membership involves joining with other members of a particular assembly in order to fulfill a certain responsibility. This is done so that the full body might function as the head intended it to function.

> Membership does not mean your only responsibilities are to sit, soak, and sour.

To become a member of a local church or small group is to be identified and functionally involved with a body of believers who are learning to live together underneath the lordship and rulership of Jesus Christ.

Membership does not mean your only responsibilities are to sit, soak, and sour. Your sole contribution is not to warm a pew or show up to various events. Rather, to be a member is to be identified and functionally involved with a group of Christians who are aligning themselves underneath Jesus Christ. This is done both locally and globally.

You can connect with other Christians as a member of a small group, online group, missions experience, nonprofit organization ...any number of ways. The local church is the primary point of connection for the body of Christ, but you can experience the benefits and responsibilities of membership in other places too.

Through these verses, we understand that we can maximize our relationship with God by being attached to others. If you're detached from the other members of the body of Christ, you're probably restricting the flow of God's relationship with you.

Let me illustrate this through a graphic visual. If I were to chop off my hand and set it on the pulpit while I went on preaching, the fact that my hand is located in the same building with my body would be meaningless. Both my hand and my body would lose. My hand would lose because it wouldn't get the benefit of the rest of my body and especially the flow of the blood it needed. And the rest of my body would lose because it wouldn't get the benefit of my hand. Disconnecting my hand from the rest of my body would hurt both— even if they were still in the same vicinity.

Friend, just showing up at church does not mean you are benefiting from Jesus Christ and His presence in your life. You could be in the vicinity of the body without being connected to it. If that happens, you will lose out on the benefits Christ wants to give you through others, and others will lose out on the benefits He wants to give them through you.

The flow of God's Spirit requires connection—our vertical connection with Him as well as our horizontal connection with one another.

God has given each of us something to contribute to the greater good. We read in 1 Corinthians 12:7, "But to each one is given the manifestation of the Spirit for the common good." The Holy Spirit is like the blood flowing through the body. He shares God's life with the various parts. But if a hand is disconnected from an arm, it no longer receives the flow of life. You and I don't receive the full manifestation of the Spirit in our lives when we are disconnected from one another. The flow of God's Spirit requires connection—our vertical connection with Him as well as our horizontal connection with one another.

> For even as the body is one and yet has many members, and all the members of the body, though they are many, are one body, so also is Christ. For by one Spirit we were all baptized into one body, whether Jews or Greeks, whether slaves or free, and we were all made to drink of one Spirit.

> For the body is not one member, but many. If the foot says, "Because I am not a hand, I am not a part of the body," it is not for this reason any the less a part of the body. And if the ear says, "Because I am not an eye, I am not a part of the body," it is not for this reason any less a part of the body. If the whole body were an eye, where would the hearing be? If the whole were hearing, where would the sense of smell be? But now God has placed the members, each one of them, in the body, just as He desired. If they were all one member, where would the

body be? But now there are many members, but one body (verses 12-20).

This is a perfect illustration of how we are made to function because it is something we can all understand. If the whole body were an eye, we wouldn't be able to hear. If the whole body were an ear, we wouldn't be able to see. Each part is essential if the body is to function as a whole.

Your Vital Role

Friend, you are a critically important member of the body of Christ. You are a vital element of God's overarching plan. If you were to disconnect yourself from others in Christ's body, you would feel the loss, and so would we. The only place you see dismembered body parts moving around and doing their own thing is in a horror film. The church was not designed to scare people but to reveal God's love to them.

It takes all of the members of the body to make up the body. Just ask anyone with type 1 diabetes how important the pancreas is. Or ask anyone on dialysis how important the kidneys are. Ask any blind person or deaf person how important the eyes or ears are, and you will get a greater understanding of how important you are to the other members of the body of Christ.

The church is not merely a place to hear sermons or sing songs. The church is to be an environment where people can be linked to one another. It is a place where we connect horizontally to carry out our various roles while experiencing a deeper vertical connection with God in our lives.

> Our unity with Jesus Christ is fleshed out
> in our unity with one another.

The Bible says that if believers aren't willing to bear one another's burdens—if they aren't willing to function as the family of God—then they think they are something that they are not, and they deceive themselves (Galatians 6:2-3). Our unity with Jesus Christ is fleshed out in our unity with one another, and this is critical for the plan of God. If you are not investing in the lives of others, you are limiting your experiential connection with God. If you are not working to promote the well-being of other Christians, you have chosen to limit God's flow to you. We are a family—you are not an only child in this home.

Parents with one child have to be intentional about teaching their children to share. Otherwise, those kids will become spoiled. But God doesn't have any "only" children. His family has many members, and He has uniquely gifted them all through His Spirit to benefit one another. Therefore it is absolutely critical that believers connect to one another. It is also critical that we continue learning to value each other more and more.

Hidden but Invaluable

I appreciate the value, respect, and gratitude that our congregation shows to me. I feel the encouragement on a regular basis, and there are many days when that very encouragement is what keeps me on pace. But we must realize that in Christ's body, each one of us is valuable. Each one of us is essential.

When you go to the doctor because something is wrong, he often ends up focusing on something you can't even see. Something on the inside was off-kilter, and that was causing symptoms on the outside. Similarly, athletes often experience pain in one part of their body when the cause of the pain is in another part entirely. The different parts of the body are connected in amazing ways.

///

There is no big "I" and little "you" in the body of Christ.

\\\\\\\\\\\\\\\\\\\\\\\\\\\\\\\\\\\\\

Just because everyone isn't up front preaching or singing or leading classes doesn't make anyone less valuable than anyone else in the body of Christ. Whether our work is up front or behind the scenes, God has gifted each of us in a way that makes each one of us important to the greater whole. We have different responsibilities and job descriptions, but every member of the body must be viewed as valuable. There is no big "I" and little "you" in the body of Christ. Just as in biology, technology, food, and the like, the visible parts often depend on the invisible parts to work at all.

I'm sure God would be happy if you sent me a note of encouragement, shook my hand, or said a kind word. And I'd like that too. But God says that the way you treat those who don't have notoriety— those who don't demonstrate a visible impact in your life—is akin to the way you treat Him. "Truly I say to you, to the extent that you did it to one of these brothers of Mine, even the least of them, you did it to Me" (Matthew 25:40). This verse seems to indicate that Christ pays special attention to the way we treat those who do not appear to have a significant role in the world's eyes.

Unfortunately, many churches appear to function more like a fraternity, sorority, or social club than the body of Christ. People relate to others who share their status or have similar roles, but they fail to truly connect with one another. Friend, that's not the church that Jesus Christ came to build. The first-century church struggled with the same problem. In James 2:1-4, we see that when the poor came into the church, they were seated in the back. But when the rich came into the church, they were seated in the front. James doesn't call that Sociology 101—he calls it sin. None of us are to look down on any others because of class, culture, race, or position. As members of one body, we are all valuable to each other.

Satan wants to destroy our unity because He knows that if we are disconnected, we will restrict God's involvement in our lives. God, by His very nature, is a unified Being. So when we are fussing and fighting all the time, or when we are neglecting others in His body, we are not modeling His image in which we were created. This impacts our relationship with God. It impacts it so much that the Bible says that if a husband and wife are not getting along with each other, understanding and valuing each other, the husband's prayers will be hindered (1 Peter 3:7).

This principle and truth—that our horizontal relationship with others impacts the experience of our vertical relationship with God— shows up repeatedly throughout Scripture. Yet we don't often talk about it or address it in our books, sermons, or lessons, or the like. And as a result, we can miss out on the full manifestation of God's presence in our individual lives, families, churches, communities ...even in our nation.

Paul emphasizes the value God places on each of us in 1 Corinthians 12:24-26.

> But God has so composed the body, giving more abundant honor to that member which lacked, so that there may be no division in the body, but that the members

may have the same care for one another. And if one member suffers, all the members suffer with it; if one member is honored, all the members rejoice with it.

The Christian life is to be all about caring.

The goal of our connectivity is summed up in these words—we are to "care for one another." The Christian life is to be all about caring. You can't keep track of every member of the entire body of Christ, and neither can I. That's why Paul tells us to care for one another. We are each to care for those around us—those God puts in our paths. When each of us is connected to someone else, and that someone else is connected to another someone else, ultimately the entire body is connected and cared for.

What does caring for others include? Listening, helping, praying, joining in a small group...any number of things. But none of that can happen until you take the risk to intentionally connect with other members of Christ's body. When you connect with the family of God, you are positioned to experience more in your relationship with Him.

I always look forward to going on a cruise with my wife. Life on a cruise ship is awesome—everything is taken care of for you. Your bags are taken to your room, your food is always ready and available, and entertainment is all around. You can come and go as you please. You don't have to do much of anything on a cruise but rest.

But the church of God is not a cruise ship. It's not a place where members are to show up and say, "Sing to me, preach to me, serve me, pray for me…but don't ask me to do anything for you." No, the church is not an ocean liner. In fact, the church is more like a battleship. We are in a war with an enemy who wants to thwart the advancement of God's kingdom on earth. And on a battleship, you need all hands on deck. Everyone on the ship has a job to do—everyone plays a part. In the same way, everyone needs to play a part in the family of God.

If you are a finger in the body of Christ, be the best finger you can be. If you are a hand, be a great hand. If you are an artery, be an awesome artery. We all need each other to be Christ's hands, feet, eyes, ears…the fully functioning body of Christ.

6

ACCEPTING
ONE ANOTHER

The American experience is unique, intriguing, exciting...and challenging. It had a singular beginning—welcoming all who wanted to come, regardless of background, ancestry, or culture. The doors of America swung wide open to all. The Statue of Liberty greeted the tired and the poor as they sought new beginnings. Those who came shared a common desire—to be free. The American experiment has always been, at its core, an experiment in freedom.

Almighty God has offered an even greater welcome. In the words of hymn writer Philip Bliss, it states simply but clearly, "Whosoever will may come." It is the offer of salvation to any and all regardless of class, culture, history, or gender. God's welcome mat says, "Whoever believes in Him shall not perish, but have eternal life" (John 3:16). People from all backgrounds have accepted Christ's invitation to be saved.

This truly is the message of salvation—that all are forgiven through faith in the death, burial, and resurrection of Jesus Christ. But like the American experience, life with God includes some challenges. We have come from many diverse backgrounds, so differences are sure to arise among us. We join together in Christ, but far too often, we end up looking at each other and thinking, "Where did you come from?"

Couples often have a similar experience. Before they get married, they are deliriously happy. But after living together day in and day out, they begin to notice their differences and even focus on them. If they don't handle this process well, their happiness may dissipate into conflict. The husband may look at his wife and say, "I didn't know you were like that!" and vice versa. Well, friends, your mate was always like that—you just hid your differences from each other while you were dating! But when you came together under the umbrella of marriage, that closeness of life on life revealed some things that ultimately led to friction and challenges.

> If we don't handle our differences
> well, they can easily divide us.

Each of us in the body of Christ has a distinctive personality. We each have a unique background and set of preferences and idiosyncrasies. This diversity brings a greater variety and strength to the body of Christ. However, if we don't handle our differences well, they can easily divide us.

When God brought us together into one big family, He joined together people who have a variety of likes and dislikes, interests, dreams, and baggage. He also asked us not only to get along but also to love one another. The apostle Paul wrote, "There is neither Jew nor Greek, there is neither slave nor free man, there is neither male nor female; for you are all one in Christ Jesus" (Galatians 3:28). We came to Christ as Jew, Greek, slave, free, male, female, and more, but in Him, we have been joined together as one new man (Ephesians 2:15).

Even with our different backgrounds, histories, preferences, and the like, God has asked us to live, worship, and work together—to love each other—while operating in unity in the family of God. In order to do that, we have to understand and embrace this next admonition to us from the apostle Paul. We've all heard it and recited it, but the myriad of rifts among us reveal that precious few of us have actually lived it out. Paul writes, "Therefore, *accept one another*, just as Christ also accepted us to the glory of God" (Romans 15:7).

It is as simple and as difficult as that. We are called as brothers and sisters in Christ to accept one another just as Christ accepted us. Accepting one another is a critical choice each of us must make if we are to celebrate and enjoy the freedom we have in the Lord. Freedom is the release from illegitimate bondage. It empowers you to become everything God created you to be.

God told Adam and Eve they could eat freely from every tree in the Garden of Eden except the tree of the knowledge of good and evil. They had plenty of other trees to choose from whenever they wanted. They had abundant freedom with limited regulation. The only thing they couldn't do was eat from one specific tree. If they messed with that tree, they would experience dire consequences. Outside of that, they were free.

Thus freedom has always been built into God's created order just as it is built into our lives as new creations in Jesus Christ. As believers, we are free to do and be many things, yet some Christians feel handcuffed because other people in the body of Christ try to tighten their restrictions and limit their freedoms. These legalistic believers add rules where none existed. They add restrictions that God never included in His commands. Like the Pharisees, they add to what God has said, and they do it in God's name.

Yes, God has rules, and He has been clear about these just as He was clear to Adam and Eve about not eating from one tree in the middle of the garden. But we become legalistic when we add to the regulations that our Lord has put in place, and we become judgmental when we condemn ourselves or others for not living up to those unrealistic expectations.

In Romans 14, Paul shows that we must follow our conscience and allow others to follow theirs. In verse 1 he writes, "Now accept the one who is weak in faith, but not for the purpose of passing judgment on his opinions." Paul opens with this blanket statement of acceptance. He admonishes us to accept others whose faith may not be as strong as our own and not to put them down or judge them.

The question is, what does it mean to accept one another? What does that look like? This is a critical question to answer because acceptance can transform individuals, families, and entire churches. In fact, many families that don't stay together could have overcome their problems if they had learned how to accept each other. Likewise, many churches don't thrive or impact their communities because they fail to teach and apply this all-important principle of acceptance.

To accept one another is to avoid judging others based on your own personal preferences.

I've been in the ministry long enough to know that people can sometimes come across as if their main mission in life is to critique others or to change them. But in Romans 14, Paul gives us three truths about accepting one another that can transform lives, homes, and churches.

Do Not Judge Opinions

To accept one another is to avoid judging others based on your own personal preferences. We find this principle at the end of Romans 14:1, where Paul says we are to accept others, "but not for the purpose of passing judgment on his opinions." Now, I want to point out that Paul is not talking about a lack of judgment entirely. Look closely— he specifically says we are not to pass judgment on someone's opinions. That's a specific kind of judgment.

We are not being told that we cannot judge sin or distinguish between right and wrong according to God's clearly defined commandments. Rather, we are not to judge people's personal preferences. People like to do things in certain ways, and their ways may be different from ours. We are not free to judge them for their preferences and opinions. God has not regulated these, so we cannot judge them as right or wrong. In other passages, the Bible teaches us that we do need to make certain judgments. But here, Paul is instructing us about what *not* to judge—people's opinions and preferences—and he gives us a concrete example.

> One person has faith that he may eat all things, but he who is weak eats vegetables only. The one who eats is not to regard with contempt the one who does not eat, and the one who does not eat is not to judge the one who eats, for God has accepted him. Who are you to judge the servant of another? To his own master he stands or falls; and he will stand, for the Lord is able to make him stand (Romans 14:2-4).

Many of the believers Paul was writing to came from backgrounds that included worshipping idols by sacrificing food to them. In fact, finding meat in the markets that had *not* been sacrificed to idols was difficult. When these people came to Christ, some of them believed that nothing was unclean in itself—including meat (this was Paul's opinion). Others felt that if they ate meat that had been sacrificed to idols, they would still be participating in the worship of those idols.

Problems arose when those who were free to eat meat sat down to eat with those who weren't. The meat eaters judged the vegetarians for not living in freedom, and the vegetarians judged the meat eaters for worshipping idols. Each group looked down on the other with contempt. Paul reminded both groups to follow their conscience but not to impose their opinions on others.

The next example Paul gave involved special days.

> One person regards one day above another, another regards every day alike. Each person must be fully convinced in his own mind...But you, why do you judge your brother? Or you again, why do you regard your brother with contempt? For we will all stand before the judgment seat of God (verses 5,10).

In other words, if a day is special to you, let it be special to you. But you don't need to force everyone else to make it special too.

My late father-in-law did not celebrate Christmas. He said we didn't know if it was actually Christ's birth date. He also said it had become so secularized that it didn't carry the meaning that a day set apart for Jesus Christ should. That being so, my wife, Lois, did not grow up celebrating Christmas. Instead, her family made a big deal about New Year's.

Our different backgrounds and histories have created different value systems.

The family I was raised in celebrated Christmas. My parents didn't have an issue with it, so in our home, celebrating Christmas was as normal as eating dinner. It was expected. However, we didn't make a big deal out of New Year's at all. When Lois and I came together and formed our own family, we decided to raise our kids celebrating Christmas, but we agreed not to pressure her parents or siblings to join in. We knew that was against their conscience, so we celebrated our way but gave them the grace not to. In addition, we often celebrated New Year's with them out of respect for what they valued as well.

Paul's words to the Romans make clear that our different backgrounds and histories have created different value systems. We are not to impose our values on others who may have their own preferences or rationale for why they believe the way they do. Much of the confusion that we face in the body of Christ today is the result of a clash of backgrounds and histories rather than a clash of doctrinal beliefs. But Paul makes it clear that we are free to hold to our preferential values without imposing those values on others or looking down on them because their values are different from ours. Paul's examples—food and holidays—aren't problem areas for most of us today, but we do have differing opinions about plenty of other things, including dancing, entertainment, spending, clothing, and drinking. Yet what the Bible does not specifically condemn, you are free to enjoy. But you are not to condemn someone else whose freedom looks different from yours.

When you go to the airport, you see all kinds of bags—soft-sided bags, hard-sided bags, tall bags, short bags, suitcases, suit bags...all sorts of things. When you go to the gate to board the plane, you will see an assortment of carry-ons—purses, briefcases, backpacks, and the like. However, there is always one standard for what goes on board. That standard is usually a place to measure your bag and a sign that says, "It must fit in here." Whatever people take on the plane must fit in that standard.

God has given us His standards in Scripture. He's given us commands, laws, and truths in His Word. We are free to hold our own preferences and opinions as long as they conform to those standards and fit within those boundaries. That brings a huge relief because we are no longer trying to please a million different people with a million different standards. Rather, we are free to live by God's standards in the way that is best for each of us. This sets us free to accept ourselves and others.

To accept others is to welcome them positively, joyfully, and kindly. It is to embrace them even when they don't do things you like, or do things the way you like, or relate to you the way you like. They are free to do what they believe is right. Regardless of the differences between their preferences and yours, you are to accept them just as God in Christ has accepted you.

///

Transforming someone's life is the Holy
Spirit's job, not yours or mine.

\\\

One of the quickest ways for husbands and wives to kill their relationship is by trying to change each other. Differences exist, as do preferences. The Lord never said, "Change one another." Rather, we are told to accept one another. We are not all at the same place in our spiritual or emotional growth. In fact, Paul points out that one person may have what is considered to be "weak faith." We are all growing at different levels. So none of us are in a position to pass judgment or try to change someone else. Only God knows where He wants us to be in relation to Him. Transforming someone's life is the Holy Spirit's job, not yours or mine.

Do Not Be a Stumbling Block

Paul continues, "Therefore let us not judge one another anymore, but rather determine this—not to put an obstacle or a stumbling block in a brother's way" (Romans 14:13). He later adds, "It is good not to eat meat or to drink wine, or to do anything by which your brother stumbles" (verse 21).

What does Paul mean when he tells us not to put an obstacle or a stumbling block in another believer's path? He means we are not to cause others to trip spiritually. A stumbling block is anything that causes someone to trip when walking, so a spiritual stumbling block causes someone to trip spiritually.

You and I are to refrain from doing things that cause other brothers or sisters in Christ to regress rather than progress in their spiritual life. This includes things that even may not be sinful themselves. For example, I don't drink wine—not because I don't have the right to, and not because I believe drinking in moderation is a sin. Rather, because of my role as a pastor and leader in the body of Christ, I have decided not to drink any alcohol simply because some people could stumble spiritually if they saw their pastor drinking.

When people see the way you live, do they take a step backward spiritually, or do they move forward?

That's a simple example, but many other things besides eating and drinking can cause our fellow members in Christ's body to stumble. Our appearance, our speech, our spending, our entertainment, our use of free time...The issue isn't whether those things are wrong. The question is, when people see the way you live, do they take a step backward spiritually, or do they move forward?

Why is this important? Paul tells us the answer.

> For if because of food your brother is hurt, you are no longer walking according to love. Do not destroy with your food him for whom Christ died. Therefore do not let what is for you a good thing be spoken of as evil; for the kingdom of God is not eating and drinking, but righteousness and peace and joy in the Holy Spirit (Romans 14:15-17).

This does not mean you can never do these things at all. It means you definitely do not do them when and where they will have a negative spiritual impact on others. We ought to care so much for one another that we will try to help one another move forward and not fall backward.

You may feel free to do something that your brother or sister in Christ feels is wrong. Accept them where they are and don't try to stuff your freedom down their throat or rub it in their face. My oldest daughter, Chrystal, did just that when she no longer had to nap every day but her younger siblings still did. She was free, but they were not. One time I caught her sneaking to the bedroom where they were napping and saying, "Nah-ne-nah-ne-nah-nah!" Chrystal was using her freedom to tick off everyone else. That's exactly what we are *not* supposed to do according to Scripture.

The kingdom of God is righteousness, peace, and joy in the Holy

Spirit. That includes accepting each other where we are at and not trying to impose our values or freedoms on others.

Do Not Cause Others to Violate Their Conscience

Our final principle in this chapter has to do with our internal guide, our conscience.

> The faith which you have, have as your own conviction before God. Happy is he who does not condemn himself in what he approves. But he who doubts is condemned if he eats, because his eating is not from faith; and whatever is not from faith is sin (Romans 14:22-23).

Violating your conscience indicates a lack of faith.

The Holy Spirit serves as our conscience in our lives. He can be compared in some ways to the metal detector we pass through at the airport, which picks up on anything that should not be there. Everyone has a conscience, but just like the metal detector at the airport, it can be set at varying levels of sensitivity. So we all don't share exactly the same convictions, nor does our conscience convict each of us on the same level. The point then is to notice when your conscience convicts you or when someone else's conscience convicts them. Violating that conscience indicates a lack of faith.

Violating the conscience grieves the Holy Spirit, which causes disruption in our lives. As Paul already established, eating meat was not sinful. Rather, it was the violation of the conscience that was sinful.

How can you know whether you feel free to do something? Ask yourself, "Can I give thanks to God for what I am doing?"

You probably remember the popular movie *Chariots of Fire*. This true story chronicled the life of Eric Liddell, the Olympic athlete whose conscience would not allow him to race on a Sunday. That was his conviction—whether it was biblically sound was not for anyone to say. His conscience dictated that he not run, so he did not run. Even though the weight of an entire nation was riding on him for a gold, he chose to honor God by honoring his conscience. If you know the story, you know that Liddell went on to win a gold medal after all on another day in another race. God honored Liddell for honoring Him first.

As you gather with fellow believers—in churches, homes, small groups, Sunday school classes, ministry teams, work teams, and the like—keep these three principles at the forefront of your mind. Respect people's preferences, keep their path free of stumbling blocks, and honor each person's conscience. As you do these things, you'll find yourself accepting others wherever they are at in life. Your horizontal representation of Jesus will be a blessing to them, it will glorify God, and it will open the door for you to experience even more in your vertical relationship with Him.

7

WELCOMING
ONE ANOTHER

When people walk up to your front door, what's the first thing they notice? If your home is like many others, the first thing strangers see may actually be a lie.

It's just one word, often painted on a pretty plaque or woven into a doormat—"Welcome."

Displaying the word "welcome" is the polite and appropriate thing to do. But to welcome someone is to joyfully invite them in. Is that really what we intend? What if we're busy? What if the person is there to sell us something we don't want? What if we're home alone and unsure of the person's motives? In these situations, we're more likely to limit the visitor's "welcome" to the front porch or perhaps the entryway, and even then for just a short time.

Suppose we do invite the person in. What happens next? Often, we tell a second lie—"Make yourself at home." If we were perfectly honest, we might say, "Sit here for a few minutes." We probably wouldn't want our visitors to poke around in our messy rooms, help themselves to whatever is in the fridge, or take a snooze in the bedroom of their choice.

The welcome we find in Scripture isn't like the welcome sign we hang on our front doors. It's not merely a word with little substance or significance. Rather, a biblical welcome is a major tenet of our teachings on the "one anothers." It's a spirit of hospitality that we can weave into our relationships with each other.

Keep in mind as we go through this study of the "one anothers" in the Bible that our personal, vertical relationship with God is intimately connected to our interpersonal, horizontal relationships with one another. A breach in our horizontal relationships can limit our experience of our vertical relationship.

God has created us to be the hands and feet of Jesus Christ. This is not a mere request from God the Father. His original design for the church, the body of Christ, is for us to live out the life of Christ—to be a horizontal Jesus to one another.

If the enemy can disconnect us from each other, he can limit what we receive from God and our experience of God because God has intentionally connected our vertical relationship with our horizontal relationships. As we saw earlier, "The one who does not love does not know God, for God is love" (1 John 4:8). In other words, the one who disconnects from a brother or sister in Christ does not experience a full connection with God because God Himself is love, and loving includes caring, connecting, encouraging, accepting...and welcoming.

What Does "Welcome" Mean?

In 1 Peter 4:9, the apostle Peter says, "Be hospitable to one another without complaint." Peter envisions the family of God as a hospitable environment where "welcome" is not just a word or a pleasantry, but a way of life. The Greek word translated "be hospitable" means to fondly receive a guest or to graciously welcome a stranger. It's more than saying kind words, although it involves that. It also includes an action and an attitude. As we'll discover in this chapter, biblical welcoming contains all three—articulation, action, and attitude.

When we welcome others, we get blessed too.

When we practice hospitality as an expression of the Christian life, God blesses others through us. But did you know that when we welcome others, we get blessed too? Here's how.

As human beings born with a sin nature, we are all prone to selfishness. Have you ever noticed that children don't have to be taught how to be selfish? This character defect comes naturally to them and to each of us. We don't have to practice being selfish—we're good at it from day one. And unfortunately, unless we do something about it, we get better and better at it as we grow older.

In God's kingdom, we receive life by giving it away.

But like every other sin, selfishness is an illusion. We think we're making life a little more enjoyable by getting what we want. But we're actually hurting ourselves. We're cutting ourselves off from the flow of life God wants to pour into us and out to others. That's where hospitality comes in. By connecting with others in this way, we open the channel of God's blessing to flow through us to them. In God's kingdom, we receive life by giving it away.

Many folks don't attend worship *service* on Sundays. Rather, they attend worship *selfish*. They come to be blessed, encouraged, inspired, forgiven, prayed for...with no thought of serving anyone else. Yet Paul tells us, "So then, while we have opportunity, let us do good to all people, and especially to those who are of the household of the faith" (Galatians 6:10). Read that again and notice what it *didn't* say. It didn't say we are to "*receive* good from all people" but rather to "*do* good to all people." The word "do" is an action word, and it clearly underlines the intentionality we are to have as members of the body of Christ to be the hands and feet of Jesus to one another.

This is not a passive call to kindness but rather an active call to engagement. It means seeking out occasions that God brings your way to warmly welcome others, or to show hospitality to them. As Paul writes, "Let love be without hypocrisy...contributing to the needs of the saints, practicing hospitality" (Romans 12:9,13).

This principle is so important that Paul includes hospitality in his list of qualifications for leaders in the church (1 Timothy 3:2). He also writes that a widow may receive financial assistance from the church only if she has "a reputation for good works; and if she has brought up children, if she has shown hospitality to strangers, if she has washed the saints' feet, if she has assisted those in distress, and if she has devoted herself to every good work" (1 Timothy 5:10).

///

Christian fellowship is characterized by people
serving others and meeting their needs.

\\\\\\\\\\\\\\\\\\\\\\\\\\\\\\\\\\

Hospitality was an expected way of life in first-century Christian culture. People were to open their hearts and demonstrate their attitude by their actions. Christianity was more than a handshake, a pat on the back, and the words "God bless you." True Christian fellowship is characterized by people serving others and meeting their needs. Sometimes, where appropriate, that includes meeting the needs of people you don't know.

This is one way the Lord breaks us out of a cycle of selfishness. He has established the family of God, His church, where we can continually practice hospitality with each other. The church is to be an extended spiritual family where hospitality becomes the norm, not the exception.

You've probably been to places with poor hospitality. I know I have. A restaurant may look nice or have great food, but if the host and servers have a bad attitude—if they are impatient or unwilling to answer your questions—you probably won't go back. Even if the food is tasty, if the staff isn't welcoming—if they don't act as if they even want you there—you're not likely to return.

God indicates that hospitality, or a spirit of selflessness, ought to mark the horizontal relationships in the church. Biblical hospitality, or welcoming others in an authentic way, begins with a servant's heart. Keep in mind that when you serve or welcome people who are likely to do things for you in return, that's called a business deal. That's not true, biblical hospitality. It's a win-win deal. But when you do something for someone else and expect nothing in return, that's the kind of hospitality that the apostle Paul says we are to be about.

Welcoming Jesus

Jesus brings this home when He equates doing things for others (horizontally) with doing things for Him (vertically).

> Then the King will say to those on His right, "Come, you who are blessed of My Father, inherit the kingdom

prepared for you from the foundation of the world. For I was hungry, and you gave Me something to eat; I was thirsty, and you gave Me something to drink; I was a stranger, and you invited Me in; naked, and you clothed Me; I was sick, and you visited Me; I was in prison, and you came to Me." Then the righteous will answer Him, "Lord, when did we see You hungry, and feed You, or thirsty, and give You something to drink? And when did we see You a stranger, and invite You in, or naked, and clothe You? When did we see You sick, or in prison, and come to You?" The King will answer and say to them, "Truly I say to you, to the extent that you did it to one of these brothers of Mine, even the least of them, you did it to Me" (Matthew 25:34-40).

Hospitality is caring for Jesus, not just caring for the person in front of you. It is somewhat similar to the popular saying that was often worn on bracelets years ago—What Would Jesus Do? To be a horizontal Jesus to others is to model what Christ would do for them, and that also demonstrates your love for God as well.

So we can ask ourselves these questions: What does Jesus think about my attitude right now? What are my actions communicating right now? Am I treating people the way I would treat Jesus if He were standing here? Instead of asking What Would Jesus Do, ask yourself, what would I do if this person in front of me were Jesus?

Jesus's story of the good Samaritan in Luke 10 provides one of our best examples of hospitality. A traveler fell on hard times, but two religious people walked by at different times, and both ignored him. They did absolutely nothing. A Samaritan—a religious outcast—was the only one who actually did something, and so Jesus called him the real neighbor.

In James 2:15-17, we are reminded that if someone shows up at your door, hungry and in need, and you simply tell him to be warm and filled, you are not fulfilling God's command of love. After all, what good is theology with no feet? What good is a belief system with no practice? Hospitality doesn't just say, "Praise the Lord, welcome." It is not just verbiage. Hospitality is the active and responsible meeting of the needs of another who comes across your path. It should be the standard and identifying mark of the family of God.

Now, I know that we live in difficult days. I know that not everyone who appears on your doorstep can be trusted and that some people will game you if they can. I realize that some people will hurt you or take advantage of you. That's why you and I need the wisdom of the Holy Spirit in practicing hospitality. I am not suggesting that you never vet your charity or that you welcome everyone irresponsibly, risking your safety and the well-being of your family and loved ones. I understand that we live in evil days.

But I don't want to rewrite the Bible simply because we live in difficult times. In fact, many of the believers in biblical times were having their lives threatened, so they, too, needed to ask God for wisdom as they welcomed strangers.

Blessing Others and Being Blessed

We certainly cannot refuse to offer hospitality simply because it's difficult or because some people may not be grateful. Hebrews 13:1-2 gives us one reason—"Let love of the brethren continue. Do not neglect to show hospitality to strangers, for by this some have entertained angels without knowing it." The Greek word translated "angels" in this verse can refer to one of two things. It was used of angelic beings—spirit beings. But the same word was also used of human messengers.

These verses reveal an important benefit of offering hospitality. One of the ways God sends you a messenger is in the context of hospitality. When you are praying for God to answer a prayer, He will sometimes respond to that prayer in a context of community. Or when you ask God to deliver you, He will often do this as you are busy welcoming others—even people you don't know very well.

For example, Abraham welcomed some strangers into his home in the hills above Sodom and Gomorrah. Little did he know that they were actually angels sent by God so Abraham could intercede for his relatives before the cities were destroyed. Time and time again, we see examples of God sending a message through someone in the context of hospitality.

///

We are better able to hear vertically from
the Lord when we live as a horizontal
Jesus, showing hospitality to others.

\\\\\\\\\\\\\\\\\\\\\\\\\\\\\\\\\\\\

God did just that in a very important time in my own life nearly four decades ago. My wife and I had been praying about a decision—should I take a teaching job at Dallas Theological Seminary as I continued working on my doctorate, or should we start a church instead? We had gathered around the dinner table with a number of people, and both Lois and I heard the answer to our prayer come out of someone's mouth so clear that we turned and looked at each other immediately. The conversation wasn't about planting churches or what I should do with my career, but God used that conversation to bring us the answer we had been seeking Him for.

We are better able to hear vertically from the Lord when we live as a horizontal Jesus, showing hospitality to others.

Deuteronomy 24:19 reveals another benefit we receive when we welcome others. "When you reap your harvest in your field and have forgotten a sheaf in the field, you shall not go back to get it; it shall be for the alien, for the orphan, and for the widow, in order that the LORD your God may bless you in all the work of your hands." In other words, when you are kind enough to welcome and share with someone else—even a stranger in need—God will be kind enough to "bless you in all the work of your hands." By increasing what you do for others horizontally, you open the doors for God to increase what He does for you vertically.

We can receive tremendous blessings when we show hospitality in the midst of our own personal want or need.

A spirit of hospitality ought to mark each of us as a believer in Jesus Christ. That's not to say that there aren't going to be days when you need some alone time. But we are talking about a spirit, an attitude of availability to one another. As we read in 1 Peter 4:9, "Be hospitable to one another without complaint." "Without complaint" indicates the spirit and the heart of the matter. That doesn't mean everything will be perfect and you need to be the perfect host. After all, hospitality is a gift, and some people excel at it. But we all can check our spirits to see whether we have a heart to give and share, or a grumbling and selfish mindset. Let a spirit of hospitality fill your heart and motivate you to practical service.

Sharing from our Need

We can receive tremendous blessings when we show hospitality in the midst of our own personal want or need. The story of the widow of Zarephath illustrates this like no other story does. As we saw in chapter 1, the prophet Elijah asked this widow for food, and she replied that she was down to one last, small meal for herself and her son. She told Elijah that after that meal, she and her son would prepare to die of starvation.

Nevertheless, when Elijah asked her for some of the bread, she agreed to share. Elijah's request seemed ridiculous given her circumstances, but she said yes anyway. Her circumstances demanded that she save her food for her and her son, but she stepped out in faith and showed hospitality to a stranger. She gave her last bit of food to the prophet. As a result, "she...and her household ate for many days. The bowl of flour was not exhausted nor did the jar of oil become empty, according to the word of the LORD which He spoke through Elijah" (1 Kings 17:15-16).

That would be an important lesson for us to learn if that's all Scripture said about it, but it's not. In fact, this widow shows up again in the words of Jesus Christ Himself. After reading from the scroll of Isaiah in the synagogue, Jesus added this:

> There were many widows in Israel in the days of Elijah, when the sky was shut up for three years and six months, when a great famine came over all the land; and yet Elijah was sent to none of them, but only to Zarephath, in the land of Sidon, to a woman who was a widow (Luke 4:25-26).

Why does He point that out? Because in order to get to the widow of Zarephath, who was a Gentile, Elijah had to pass by the Jewish widows. What made this widow stand out more than the others? This widow was willing to trust God even in the middle of a crisis. She was willing to show hospitality to a stranger—a prophet she had never met. And when she showed hospitality, giving out of her want and not merely her excess, God saw that as an act of faith, reached down into her life, and turned her situation around.

Friend, God honors hospitality in unique ways. He recognizes the sacrifice of selflessness along with the faith of giving, and He rewards them on a number of levels. This issue is so important to God that He will show mercy to you as you show mercy to others (James 2:13). Make a priority of welcoming others and meeting the needs of those around you as a horizontal Jesus, and watch God invade your circumstances vertically with His power and might.

8

UNIFYING
WITH ONE ANOTHER

I live in Texas, the land of hot weather and fire ants. Those two things come with the territory of living in this part of our nation.

When fire ants set up shop at your home, mounds begin to appear on your lawn or near the foundation of your house. The ants build these mounds and take up residence in them on your property. They have collected themselves together and invaded your territory in order to build their little kingdom at your address. Small as they are, together they can erect impressive knolls right in the middle of your once-beautiful lawn. They are united in a common goal and empowered by it—to serve their queen.

I saw one of these ant mounds not too long ago and was reminded of the devil's plan of attack on the family of God. He seeks to build his kingdom on God's premises. You and I are firsthand witnesses of an ungodly belief system attacking our culture and promoting agendas that have nothing to do with heaven. These belief systems have even invaded some of our churches.

It's amazing how much power and impact people can have when they share a common goal. In fact, a small minority of like-minded people can make big changes. Lobbyists and protesters—even in small numbers—wield great power when unified. So we must ask ourselves, is the church of Jesus Christ experiencing the unity and exerting the national influence that we should, especially considering the strength of our numbers? Sadly, the answer is often no. Even though we claim the same God and worship the same Lord, we have allowed differences in race, class, culture, preferences, priorities, platforms, and more to divide us. In doing so, we have reduced our cultural impact as the horizontal representatives of Jesus.

Jesus stated clearly, "Any kingdom divided against itself is laid waste; and any city or house divided against itself will not stand" (Matthew 12:25). This applies not only to the universal body of Christ but also to the local church's impact on individual lives, families, marketplaces, neighborhoods, communities, and schools. Hell has sought to divide God's kingdom to minimize His influence. Satan is the ultimate divider. He tried to split up heaven by getting one-third of the angels to join him in rebellion against God. He brought chaos into the first family when he separated Adam and Eve from God and pitted them against each other. Satan also instigated sibling hatred when he enticed the first son (Cain) to kill his brother (Abel). In fact, Satan introduced so much dissension into the world that God issued a worldwide flood.

Satan loves to divide. When he divides, he can conquer. This is because he knows something about God's nature that you and I need to always remember.

The Bible is clear that God is one being. Yet that one being includes three coequal persons—God the Father, God the Son, and God the Spirit. The one God is unified in essence but distinct in personality, and we have come to refer to this tri-unity as the Trinity. The Father is not the Son, the Son is not the Father, and the Spirit is neither. Yet the three persons make up the one being—the Godhead. The best way I know how to illustrate it is with a pretzel that has three holes. Hole number one is not hole number two. And hole number two is not hole number three. But the one pretzel with the three holes is all tied together by the same dough. The "dough" that ties the Trinity together includes the divine nature and the attributes of Deity.

When people live in disunity, God backs off.

Because Satan understands the unity of God and because his goal is to keep God from being involved in your life, family, church, and culture, he crafts an agenda of division. This agenda of division is designed to keep God out of the equation. Satan knows that when people live in disunity, God backs off. So Satan makes the most of scenarios that lead to disunity. He widens the gaps between people by inflating their differences and promoting their personal agendas.

Little disagreements can turn into complete standoffs in homes, friendships, workplaces, and churches. Small misunderstandings can disrupt the unity of two people or entire groups. When people jump to conclusions and allow their emotions to flare up, healthy communication ends and heated arguments begin.

Unique in Unity

As a reminder, we have been looking at the "one anothers" found in Scripture and learning how to be the hands and feet of Jesus to each other. We have seen that the full manifestation and experience of our vertical relationship with God hinges, to a large degree, on our horizontal relationships with one another. So when the horizontal hinge is broken and the "one anothers" are not fully in place in our lives, we limit our experience of our vertical relationship with God.

Unity is not uniformity; unity is oneness of purpose.

This chapter's emphasis is on maintaining our unity with one another. What is unity? It is based on the very nature of God. Unity is not uniformity; unity is oneness of purpose. Unity is what we see when unique individuals join hands and move in a common direction. For example, an orchestra is unified not because all the instruments are the same, but because the different instruments are playing the same song. They are using their unique sounds to create beautiful harmonic textures. Another example I like to use is that of a football team. A football team isn't unified because all the positions are the same. It's unified because all the different positions are working toward a common goal. Unity requires uniqueness. To experience unity is to embrace uniqueness and welcome differences as people march together toward a common purpose.

The definition of unity is oneness of purpose, not sameness of being.

You and I should never try to squeeze people into our mold. Scripture does not instruct us to conform to one another. Rather, we are to come together as one—with all our differences—for a common purpose.

> Now may the God who gives perseverance and encouragement grant you to be of the same mind with one another according to Christ Jesus, so that with one accord you may with one voice glorify the God and Father of our Lord Jesus Christ (Romans 15:5-6).

Notice the phrases "same mind," "one accord," and "one voice." The definition of unity is oneness of purpose, not sameness of being. Like a quilt with various colors and patterns that have been blended together into a harmonious whole, a church in unity celebrates each person's unique place in the divine design.

Not only that, but unity is absolutely critical for the deepest experience of God in our lives.

Unity is so essential that Paul urges us, "Keep your eye on those who cause dissensions and hindrances contrary to the teaching which you learned, and turn away from them" (Romans 16:17). He tells us to look out for people who disrupt the unity in our lives, homes, and churches because Satan is using them to keep God out of the situation. This is never clearer than in 1 Peter 3:7: "You husbands in the same way, live with your wives in an understanding way, as with someone weaker, since she is a woman; and show her honor as a fellow heir of the grace of life, so that your prayers will not be hindered."

God is the personification of unity—so we're not likely to experience Him if we're living in disunity.

Friend, if a husband's prayer is hindered when the husband and wife are not living in unity, then what do you think Satan's goal is? Satan's goal is to bring about disunity in marriages, homes, churches, communities, and nations. Satan seeks to keep us fighting so that our prayers to God do not bring the same results they bring when our vertical relationship with God is unencumbered.

Unity is no small issue at all. To a large degree, unity affects whether God shows up or keeps His distance. God is one—He is the personification of unity—so we're not likely to experience Him if we're living in disunity.

How Do We Have Unity?

Paul makes a very clear point in his letter to the church at Ephesus on this topic of unity when he says that we are to be "diligent to preserve the unity of the Spirit in the bond of peace" (Ephesians 4:3). Some translations say that we are to "make every effort" to preserve the unity of the Spirit. The Greek word translated "bond" in Ephesians 4:3 is sometimes translated "belt." Essentially, we are told to let peace bind us together (like a belt wrapped around us) and preserve our unity.

We are not called to create unity but rather to preserve it.

The basis of our unity is the Holy Spirit, so unless the Holy Spirit is free to rule in our lives, we cannot preserve or maintain our unity. When we sin against each other—by judging, being selfish, creating division, or the like—our relationship with the Spirit is hindered, and the unity of the Spirit suffers as well.

Keep in mind that we are not called to create unity but rather to preserve it. We don't need to invent it—we just need to live in it. Unity with each other comes by God's Spirit living in us. When our horizontal relationships with each other are in order, we experience the vertical flow of the Spirit in our lives, and unity is the result.

One of the best ways we can go about maintaining our unity is to base our thoughts and decisions on the Word of God. When we use His standard as our governing rule and His kingdom agenda as our overarching goal, our differences fade into the background. Unfortunately, though, too many of us align ourselves with preachers, politicians, or platforms more than we do with God's Word. We evaluate things based on a human viewpoint rather than God's viewpoint. This is not a new phenomenon. In fact, Paul faced the same issues in his day.

> Now I exhort you, brethren, by the name of our Lord Jesus Christ, that you all agree and that there be no divisions among you, but that you be made complete in the same mind and in the same judgment. For I have been informed concerning you, my brethren, by Chloe's people, that there are quarrels among you. Now I mean this, that each one of you is saying, "I am of Paul," and "I of Apollos," and "I of Cephas," and "I of Christ." Has Christ been divided? Paul was not crucified for you, was he? Or were you baptized in the name of Paul? I thank God that I baptized none of you except Crispus and Gaius, so that no one would say you were baptized in my name (1 Corinthians 1:10-15).

Christ did not die for a denomination—
He died for each one of us.

If we want our Lord to show up with His powerful presence in the body of Christ, in our communities, and in our nation, one of the first things we need to realize is that Christ did not die for a denomination—He died for each one of us. Yes, preferences and platforms exist. However, we would be far more effective in influencing families, communities, and our culture with God's kingdom principles based on His Word if we focused on our common purpose. Consider the impact we could have if we linked platform with platform, denomination with denomination, and church with church at those strategic times when a collective impact is needed the most.

Paul resisted disunity in the church because he knew the power of unity. He was surely familiar with Christ's words...

> If two of you agree on earth about anything that they may ask, it shall be done for them by My Father who is in heaven. For where two or three are gathered together in My name, I am there in their midst (Matthew 18:19-20).

Paul also resisted disunity on the basis of race. When 11:00 on Sunday morning is still the most segregated hour in America, we in the body of Christ have a long way to go toward living out biblical unity.

Restoring Unity

Scripture shows us how to quickly fix the problem of disunity based on race, culture, ethnicity, and class. The key is to deal with it as a spiritual and theological issue rather than merely a social and political issue. Notice the way Paul responded to division in Galatians 2. This is the well-known incident in which Peter decided that it was okay to hang out with Gentile believers—that is, until the boys from his Jewish "hood" showed up.

After the Lord warned Peter against showing partiality (Acts 10:34), Peter put his new understanding into practice by crossing the railroad tracks and relating to people of a different race and a different culture. In fact, he got into this so much that he started eating with Gentile believers in Antioch. But that's exactly where the problem developed. Some of Peter's friends from the Jewish part of town in Jerusalem came down to Antioch. When they showed up, "he began to withdraw and hold himself aloof" from his Gentile brothers and sisters (Galatians 2:12).

Why did Peter do this? Evidently the Jews said something like this: "Peter, what are you doing here eating with Gentiles? Don't you know we Jews don't do that? It's against the guidelines of our race. We'll all get together in heaven, but on earth we don't have that kind of social relationship with Gentiles." So Peter stopped having fellowship with the Gentiles because he feared what his Jewish brethren would say.

That's when it got really bad. "The rest of the Jews joined him in hypocrisy, with the result that even Barnabas was carried away by their hypocrisy" (verse 13). When Peter pushed his chair back from the table and left, so did the other Jews who had previously joined him. In fact, even Barnabas got caught up in it. Barnabas was raised in Cyprus, a Gentile colony. He was raised with Gentiles, went to school with Gentiles, and played with Gentiles. But that's how bad racial divides really are. They can make good people act badly. So Barnabas followed Peter out the door.

There was only one problem—Paul saw what happened. Paul was

equally committed to his Jewish history, culture, and people, yet he publicly excoriated Peter's non-Christian action, saying that Peter was "not straightforward about the truth of the gospel" (verse 14). The key point is truth. An objective standard transcended Peter's cultural commitment.

As we apply this example to our lives, remember that even Peter—an apostle and one of Jesus's three closest friends—was not allowed to tamper with the unity of the Spirit. No one has an excuse for placing culture above Christ, or race above righteousness. God's standard still stands, and cultural preferences are never to hinder Christians from conforming to that standard. Scripture alone is the final authority by which racial relationships are determined.

Paul did what he needed to do. He didn't hold a meeting. He didn't conduct a sensitivity seminar. He didn't say, "Hey, can't we all just get along?" Nor did he offer Peter a ten-week Bible study. Paul said, "Peter, you are messing with the gospel. Stop it!" Having caved to racial pressure and the prejudice of his fellow Jews, Peter had failed the test of truth. He had left the Gentiles in order to not offend the Jews. In deference to the cultural pressure of his own race, he discredited the message of the gospel that God had so graphically conveyed to him in the home of Cornelius—a Gentile.

What is the kingdom solution to divisions in the body of Christ along class, cultural, racial, and denominational lines? Be committed to the truth. Paul said that Peter and the other Jewish believers got into trouble because they left the truth they knew, which was that in Christ "there is neither Jew nor Greek" (Galatians 3:28). They left the truth, and that's our problem today. We need more people who are willing to speak and stand for the truth. Peter was the leader of the disciples. If the leader is not willing to live out the truth, how can we expect the followers to follow the truth?

This hits us who teach the truth of God from the pulpit. A mist in the pulpit becomes a fog in the pew. Racial division has continued in this country because too many pulpits have been too quiet too long. Too many pulpits have been divided too long. Too many pulpits have sought their own individual platforms at the expense of the unity of the Spirit in the body of Christ.

Believers Without Borders

Paul concludes his recounting of the incident with the Gentiles and the Jews with what has become my life's verse. "I have been crucified with Christ; and it is no longer I who live, but Christ lives in me; and the life which I now live in the flesh I live by faith in the Son of God, who loved me and gave Himself up for me" (Galatians 2:20). In these words, Paul reminds Peter and all of us that our identity is to be in Christ alone, not culture. Whenever we allow our history, background, class, race, gender, personality, or culture to overrule God's rightful place in our thoughts, motives, and actions, we are limiting the expression of God's involvement in our lives. And we are hurting the cause of the gospel.

Unity demands humility. It requires loving one another not only across racial or denominational lines but also across class lines. Paul instructs us, "Be of the same mind toward one another; do not be haughty in mind, but associate with the lowly. Do not be wise in your own estimation" (Romans 12:16). James takes it even further.

> My brethren, do not hold your faith in our glorious Lord Jesus Christ with an attitude of personal favoritism. For if a man comes into your assembly with a gold ring and dressed in fine clothes, and there also comes in a poor man in dirty clothes, and you pay special attention to the one who is wearing the fine clothes, and say, "You sit here in a good place," and you say to the poor man, "You stand over there, or sit down by my footstool," have you not made

distinctions among yourselves, and become judges with evil motives? Listen, my beloved brethren: did not God choose the poor of this world to be rich in faith and heirs of the kingdom which He promised to those who love Him? But you have dishonored the poor man (James 2:1-6).

One of the greatest reasons God calls us to unity is so that we will be a testimony to the world of the sacrifice of Jesus Christ and the love of God the Father. Through unity we are able to live as a horizontal Jesus to those who do not yet know Him. Jesus tells us this plainly.

I do not ask on behalf of these alone, but for those also who believe in Me through their word; that they may all be one; even as You, Father, are in Me and I in You, that they also may be in Us, so that the world may believe that You sent Me (John 17:20-21).

God's glory is manifested in unity (see verses 22-23).

Unity is a greater preamble to the presentation of the gospel than anything else we could ever do.

This is the greatest rationale Scripture provides for the call to unity. Jesus asks that we may all be one—just as God is unified in the Trinity—and He follows that up with a "so that." The "so that" is there to give us the reason for the unity, and in it we see that Jesus wants the world to believe that God the Father sent Him to earth as the sacrifice for our sins. Unity is a greater preamble to the presentation of the gospel than anything else we could ever do. And disunity (as Paul so clearly pointed out in Galatians 2) is an enormous hindrance to the gospel.

Many of our churches have made evangelism a priority, and that is good. However, when we do not simultaneously elevate the need and call for unity with one another, we are not preaching or modeling the whole gospel. We have truncated the message of Jesus Christ and limited its reach to a world in need. Unity with one another must be of utmost importance as we go about the business of preaching Christ and making disciples in His name.

As long as Satan can keep us divided by our preferences, personalities, platforms, and such, we will never fully realize the presence and power of God descending on us with His miraculous power. This is not merely a topic of sociological seminars. Unity with one another is one of the most strategic aims that we in the body of Christ could ever seek to employ. Psalm 133 is one of only two places in all of Scripture where God "commanded" a blessing (the other is Deuteronomy 28:8). The criteria listed in the passage for this command is the unity of His people. How could anything be more critical and essential than the basis upon which God will command a blessing? Unity sets the stage for God to show up in full force. In Acts, the unity of the early church led to the Holy Spirit manifesting His awesome power (Acts 2; 4:23-37).

I want to experience the manifestation of heaven in history. I'm sure you do too. We all want God to show up in our homes, churches, communities, and culture. Yet God will not show up where there is illegitimate division, so we must do all we can to preserve the unity of the Spirit among us.

9

SERVING
ONE ANOTHER

Not too long ago I pulled into a gas station, filled my tank, and then went in the convenience store to pick up a bottle of water and a bag of nuts. While I was standing in line, two employees behind the counter noticed that another customer was having trouble operating one of the gas pumps outside. One of the employees decided to go out and help her.

As he walked out the door, the other employee smiled and said, "I didn't know this was a full-service gas station."

I laughed and replied, "Those things haven't been around here for a long time. I guess he's just trying to help out."

She just laughed again, mumbling under her breath as she rang up my water and peanuts, "Full-service gas station—my word! Look at him out there!"

Today, full-service gas stations have become difficult to find. Now nearly every filling station is self-service—you take care of everything yourself. I remember pulling into full-service stations and watching as employees washed the windshield, checked the oil, and even checked the tire pressure while filling the tank. All the while, I'd be relaxing in my car because the employees were there to serve the customer.

Those were the days. Now you're fortunate if the self-service machine reads your credit card and you don't have to run inside to prepay.

In my six-plus decades here on earth, I've watched as something else has become increasingly difficult to find—a full-service disciple. So often today believers simply want to be served, blessed, helped, encouraged, counseled, loved, and the like without feeling the need to serve anyone else. This is largely because of our fascination with celebrities, reality-TV stars, and red-carpet events. Each of us wants to feel significant, to be treated as someone special for a moment. In Christianity, I call this the prince and princess mentality. The Bible does in fact describe us as children of God and corulers with Christ, but we sometimes forget that other people are God's heirs too.

///

The way up the ladder is down it. The rise
to celebrity starts on your knees.

\\\

We also forget that the King of kings came to serve and to lay down His life as a ransom for many. As King, He is to be our model. We are to be a reflection of Him—a horizontal Jesus—serving one another as servants of the Most High.

In God's economy, the way up the ladder is down it. The rise to celebrity starts on your knees with a basin, a towel, and a humble heart.

The Path to Greatness

One day, Jesus's disciples were arguing about who among them was the greatest (Mark 9:33-34). Now, before we jump in and judge them, we need to remember that we do the same thing ourselves. We might not come right out and say it, but we jockey for position in our workplaces, our friendships, and our homes. It's human nature to seek significance, and we've been duped into measuring people's significance by how well-known they are.

But as Christ's disciples argued that day, He gave them—and us— the greatest insight into greatness ever offered. It's an insight that we often overlook in our teachings on humility and our emphasis on ser- vanthood. He said, "If anyone wants to be first, he shall be last of all and servant of all" (verse 35).

James and John must not have gotten the message, because on another occasion, they asked Jesus to give them places of honor in His glory. When the other disciples heard about this, they felt indignant. Jesus used the situation as a teaching moment. "Whoever wishes to become great among you shall be your servant; and whoever wishes to be first among you shall be slave of all" (Mark 10:43-44).

The point we often miss when digging into theses passages is that Jesus never condemned the disciples for wanting to be great. Nor does He condemn the desire for greatness in any of us. Rather, Christ rec- ognized this innate need, which reflects the image of God, and He directed us toward true greatness and the path to attain it.

When you serve, God recognizes
kingdom greatness in you.

"Do you want to be great?" Jesus said, in essence. "Great! Then serve, and you will be."

Service is the true path to significance. Service to others horizontally opens up your engagement with God vertically because when you serve, He recognizes kingdom greatness in you. If you want to have a more powerful, life-changing vertical experience with God, your horizontal relationships must be characterized by a servant's heart.

Paul writes, "You were called to freedom, brethren; only do not turn your freedom into an opportunity for the flesh, but through love *serve one another*" (Galatians 5:13).

If we are to develop a servant's heart, we must first discover what the word "service" means in the Bible. To serve is to focus on others and act for their benefit in the name of Christ. Service begins with a humble attitude and includes actively looking out for the interests of others. You become a true servant when you come alongside others and help them improve spiritually, physically, emotionally, or circumstantially. You serve when your actions make someone else's life better.

I've performed plenty of weddings through the decades. Shortly before the ceremony begins, I meet with the bride to offer a time of thanksgiving before the Lord and blessing on the upcoming union. Bridesmaids are often scurrying around, making sure that everything is just right. One of the bridesmaids is checking her dress, another might be checking her hair or makeup, and yet another is talking with the wedding planner to confirm that everything is on schedule. The bridesmaids are focused on one goal in these moments. They are making certain that when the bride walks down the aisle, her future husband will delight in her beauty. Bridesmaids are like dressed-up servants—they are there to support the bride any way they can.

As disciples of Christ, we serve the church, the bride of Christ. People serving people—that is beautiful to our Lord. And as we serve one another, we are helping each other prepare to meet Christ face-to-face and participate in the wedding supper of the Lamb. One of the reasons God created the church as the body of Christ was to provide a family context for our servanthood to take place.

How can you discover the purpose and destiny God has designed you to fulfill? By serving.

Yet far too often the church is seen simply as a place to receive. People come to be fed, similar to turkeys waddling in on a turkey farm, wondering who is going to feed them. The problem with turkeys is, they cannot fly. Turkeys aren't going anywhere, or if they do, they aren't going very far because all they do is eat and get fat. God has called each of us into His family—not so we will get fat, and not so we can merely waddle in and waddle out, but so that we can practice serving. In so doing, we will discover the greatness He has destined us for.

The Path to Your Destiny

How can you discover the purpose and destiny God has designed you to fulfill? By serving.

Think about the appliances in your home. Each one carries out a certain function and performs whatever it was created to do. It is there to serve you. It takes care of your needs, and it fulfills its own purpose and function. Similarly, as you serve you will discover the gifts, skills, passion, and purpose God has placed within you, and He will reveal the unique reason you were placed here on earth.

> The body of Christ is not to be made of leeches,
> or we would surely bleed to death.

As a pastor, I've seen church member after church member come through the doors into our sanctuary wanting to be served but unwilling to serve. "Preach to me, sing to me, minister to me...but don't ask me to do anything for anyone else." In the animal world, we would call that a leech. The body of Christ is not to be made of leeches, or we would surely bleed to death.

Of course, you can't serve everyone at all times. As the pastor of a church, neither can I. But each of us can serve someone. As everyone seeks to serve someone else, ultimately everyone will be served—including you.

One of my favorite books of the Bible is Ephesians. It includes one of the most revealing passages on discovering our life purpose and destiny.

> For by grace you have been saved through faith; and that not of yourselves, it is the gift of God; not as a result of works, so that no one may boast. For we are His workmanship, created in Christ Jesus for good works, which God prepared beforehand so that we would walk in them (Ephesians 2:8-10).

When this passage refers to good works, it's talking about servanthood. God has established and ordained opportunities for us to serve. If our Lord has prepared opportunities for us to carry out good works of service, we ought be excited about fulfilling them. These are not random acts of kindness He has made us for. Rather, because of

Christ's sacrificial death and atonement for our sins, grace has paved the way for the path of servanthood. Serving is one of the greatest and most tangible ways to give thanks to God for His gift of salvation.

The Motivation of Freedom

The things Christ secured for us on the cross—abundant life here and now as well as life with God forever—are to be the motivations for our service. It is the heart that drives the hands, the mindset that drives the movements. Remember that Paul said we were called to freedom. Yet we are not to use that freedom as an opportunity for the flesh, but instead as empowerment to serve one another in love (Galatians 5:13).

Far too many of us have forgotten the freedom the cross has secured, so we lack the impetus and motivation to serve. Others of us are still bound in legalism, not feeling the full effects of Christ's atonement in our lives, so service feels like an additional burden. When you and I fully grasp and appropriate the freedom that Jesus Christ has purchased on our behalf, we will finally tap into the true spirit of service.

There was a time in our nation when freedom was valued much more highly than it seems to be today. The benefits that our country provided included the freedom of expression, education, and opportunity. Due to the solid and strong protection of our government, most of our citizens experienced the ability at some level to pursue life, liberty, and happiness in the context of freedom. It was in these days that President John F. Kennedy said his famous line, "Ask not what your country can do for you; ask what you can do for your country."

Our president knew what our country had already done on behalf of the lives of so many, so he called for service. Now, our country has its flaws, but it was established on this premise of freedom. The freedom it offers is the opportunity to maximize every individual's potential to the greatest degree possible. Of course, things don't always work out that way. Nonetheless, the foundational premise remains the same. Because of this, JFK challenged us to serve in whatever capacity we can as a result of what we have gained.

If JFK's speech motivated Americans to serve their nation in gratitude for the freedom they enjoyed, how much more should Jesus's sacrifice motivate us to serve His church in gratitude for the freedom He has provided for us?

The Gift of Surrender

If I were to tell you, "There's no difference between you and me in God's plans," would you believe me?

Many Christians would stop me right there and say, "Now, hold on, Tony. You're a leader, pastor, teacher, author, and speaker. I'm not any of that."

True, I answered a call of God on my life to be a pastor, but I was called to serve Him from the day I was saved—and you were too. Some of the things He's asking me to do are highly visible, but you are no less important to His plans.

The beauty of the gospel is that God says to every one of us, "I've got a plan and purpose for you." Jeremiah 1:5 confirms that. "Before I formed you in the womb I knew you, and before you were born I consecrated you."

God didn't take you to heaven the day you were saved, so He must want you to fulfill a divine purpose here on earth.

God is mindful of us, and He has made a way for us to have fellowship with Him. He paid the price through Christ's death on the cross so that we might be saved. But that is only the beginning of the adventure. When we give our lives to God, we are all called to do good works, as we saw earlier in Ephesians 2:10. God didn't take you to heaven the day you were saved, so He must want you to fulfill a divine purpose here on earth. The truth is, you were saved to serve. God has an assignment for you.

We've got to understand that when we surrendered our hearts to Christ, it was "moving day." Ephesians 2:6 says that God seated you in the heavenly places with Christ Jesus. You moved from a life based primarily on the physical realm—taste, touch, sight, sound, and smell—to a life based primarily on the spiritual realm.

The enemy will do all he can to keep you focused on the physical realm. "It's all about you. You're the most important person. Climb the corporate ladder to get all you can. He who has the most gold wins." But when we are "seated in heavenly places" with Christ, we see we are called to God's purposes, and that means we see life through the eyes of a servant.

God is saying, "For the rest of your life on earth, I want you to yield yourself to My purposes, to My pleasure, and to My goals. I have a work for you to do. I have good works for you to do to advance My kingdom on earth." Yet many Christians remain unfulfilled, miserable, and unhappy because they've never gotten around to the work that God has for them. They've never discovered the immense reward that comes with a life of service.

A Work in Progress

Your destiny as a believer is settled. Heaven will be your home. But your life on earth, your new life with Christ, is still a work in progress. The Greek word translated "workmanship" in Ephesians 2:10

can refer to a masterpiece, such as a work of art or a beautiful poem. It was used to describe a painter or a writer using plain materials to craft something elegant.

The canvas does not tell the painter what to paint. The clay does not tell the potter what to fashion. But many Christians are trying to get God to turn them into what they want to be rather than saying, "God, turn me into what You want me to be. You are the painter, and I am the canvas; You are the potter, and I am the clay."

Jesus is our model, and He said in John 4:34, "My food is to do the will of Him who sent me and to accomplish His work." His perspective is exactly the opposite from the one you're getting from the world. We are His workmanship, and we were "created in Christ Jesus for good works." Anyone can do good things, but believers are empowered to do divinely inspired activities that glorify God and benefit others. God already had them in mind when He created you. You don't have to dream them up—they will be revealed in your spirit as you yield yourself to God. You may not have all the details, but you will feel something in your spirit when you pray.

Simply pray each day, "Lord, I'm available. Create in me the desire to do the works You have in mind for me. Let me see more of Your plan for me each day. I believe You will give me the desire to do it and the ability to pull it off." Paul wrote, "Work out your salvation with fear and trembling, for it is God who is at work in you, both to will and to work for His good pleasure" (Philippians 2:12-13).

///

You are custom-made for the service
God has for you in this life.

\\

When you are on God's assignment for service, He will give you the desire ("to will") and the ability to carry it out ("to work"). God says, "I'll do the work on your inside and change your heart. You just have to do the work on the outside. Be obedient and listen for My voice."

You are custom-made for the service God has for you in this life. Isaiah 44:2 says, "The LORD who made you and formed you from the womb...will help you." He gets the credit for your design, your purpose, and the service you do in His name. Psalm 138:8 says, "The LORD will accomplish what concerns me." He has made you with a purpose, and He's determined to fulfill it. That means you face an uphill battle if you're pushing your own agenda. But if you choose to live a life of humble service, you are on a straight path to living out your greatness.

Living in Freedom

I'm convinced that one of the main reasons we don't live a life of service is our lack of experiential freedom. I intentionally use the word "experiential" because every believer in Jesus Christ has been set free—we just don't always experience that freedom as God intended. In Galatians 5:1 we read, "It was for freedom that Christ set us free; therefore keep standing firm and do not be subject again to a yoke of slavery." Friend, Jesus Christ set you free to be free. He did not set you free so you would return to bondage. On the cross, Christ posted bail to get you out of the bondage of eternal hell and the bondage of anything that holds you back today.

Many things enslave people in the world today—addictions, challenges, spiritual blindness...sometimes the options seem endless. Other people may put "a yoke of slavery" on us, but we can also put on some of our own chains, such as legalism. Whatever handcuffs a person's mind, emotions, actions, or circumstances holds them hostage. Jesus Christ came that we might be set free, not so that we would be confined in a cell.

Many people aren't serving because they are still in jail. Jesus has set them free, but they choose to remain bound to the law. They are still trying to earn God's favor, blessings, and freedom through what they do or don't do. When they make good choices, they come to God with a spirit of entitlement, or pride. When they make poor choices, they come to Him with a spirit of guilt and shame. Either way, their hearts are not full of gratitude, so they've lost their primary motivation for service. When we lose sight of grace (Galatians 5:4) and Christ's gift of atonement, we also lose our impetus for living in the light of that grace. We lose out on the freedom to serve.

When you and I fully understand what Christ accomplished for us on the cross and the freedom God has given us, serving God and serving others will not be difficult at all.

In the movie *The Hanging Tree*, Gary Cooper plays Joseph "Doc" Frail, a medical doctor who goes about his days helping injured and sick people. In one point of the movie, Doc comes across Rune—a young man who had been shot and was bleeding to death. After digging the bullet out of him, Doc brings Rune back to life and health.

Later, when the young man is fully recovered and realizes his life has been saved, he asks the doctor how he can repay him. The doctor said something to this effect: "I'll tell you what you can do for me. You can become my assistant and help me save other people's lives. In fact, you can do this for the rest of your life because that's how long you would have been dead if I hadn't saved you."

Makes sense, doesn't it?

Do you know where you would be if God had not saved and delivered you? Do you know where you would have been had Christ not intervened on the cross? I know where I would have been. And when you truly comprehend and understand exactly what God saved you from, how He saved you, and for how long your salvation will last, serving Him doesn't become such a problem in your life anymore. Rather than seeing each occasion to serve Him as an inconvenience, you see it for what it is—an opportunity, a privilege, a passion. Every day above ground is a gift of grace from God the Father. We serve God and others during this time in humble recognition that we have been saved, delivered, and set free.

Strengthened Through Service

When athletes want to strengthen their legs, they do an exercise called a squat. They put weights on their shoulders, bend low with their knees, and straighten back up again. With each bend of the legs, their legs become stronger. Do you want to know why so many believers are not that strong? It's because so few of us are willing to bend. Few of us are willing to go low and serve. We're unwilling to carry the weight of someone else and serve those who have nothing to offer in return.

God calls us to a life of humility and service. In order to live out His desire for us, we need to bend our wants, schedules, desires, expectations, and more in order to meet other people's needs. In doing so, we will bring glory to God while strengthening our own spiritual walk and faith. We will deepen our intimacy with God and strengthen our vertical relationship with Him. Just as a waiter or a waitress will receive a greater tip for excellent service than for poor service, our Lord notices what you and I do for one another. Your service will be rewarded here on earth or in heaven (Ephesians 6:7-8; Colossians 3:23-24).

When I was growing up in Baltimore, it was a tradition to get crabs for dinner two or three times a month. I'll never forget those dinners, especially because of the way we cooked the crabs. At my house, the crabs didn't come prepared. We had to put the live crabs in a pot of boiling water to cook them. As soon as the crabs felt that heat, they tried to climb over each other to get out of that pot. But whenever one crab was about to successfully maneuver out of the pot, another crab climbed up on it and pulled it back down. Eventually they all died simply because they competed against each other to save themselves.

Now, imagine what would happen if the crabs somehow learned the secret of service. Some crabs would help the others climb out, and then those who made it would reach back down to pull out the last few.

The more we look to the interests of others, the more we will bring God glory, advance His kingdom agenda, and fulfill our personal destinies.

We are all in this thing together. We are on the same team—God's kingdom team. The more we look to the interests of others, the more we will bring God glory, advance His kingdom agenda, and fulfill our personal destinies. As the church embraces a lifestyle of serving, we will become the dynamic, transformational force we were intended to be.

The Towel

The greatest story of servanthood, outside of the cross, is set in a roomful of men with dirty feet. Shortly before Christ was to go to the cross, He gave us a living example of service.

> Jesus, knowing that the Father had given all things into
> His hands, and that He had come forth from God and

was going back to God, got up from supper, and laid aside His garments; and taking a towel, He girded Himself.

Then He poured water into the basin, and began to wash the disciples' feet and to wipe them with the towel with which He was girded (John 13:3-5).

Just as He had done throughout His earthly ministry, the Master became the slave. The Maker became the servant. Jesus donned a towel, grabbed a bucket, and washed the feet of those who in just a few hours would desert him.

This act of service may seem quaintly irrelevant in our world, but in Christ's time, washing guests' feet before dinner was standard practice. People wore makeshift sandals, they walked for transportation, and the roads were dusty, so their feet quickly became filthy in the course of everyday life. That's why a servant often positioned himself at the entrance of a home with a bucket of water and a towel—to wash the feet of the family and guests as they came in. This was a common way of saying, "Welcome."

Jesus shows us the key to serving—His actions were rooted in an authentic identity with God.

By kneeling and washing His disciples' feet, Jesus demonstrated what service ought to look like. His humble actions expressed not only His love for His friends but also His relationship with His Father. Look again at verses 3 and 4.

Jesus, knowing that the Father had given all things into His hands, and that He had come forth from God and was going back to God, got up from supper, and laid aside His garments; and taking a towel, He girded Himself.

Because Jesus fully grasped His own freedom and significance, He was able to serve. Too often, we waver in our self-worth, and as a result, we jockey for positions of honor rather than opportunities to serve. But Jesus shows us the key to serving—His actions were rooted in an authentic identity with God.

//

The higher our worldly position, the lower we should bend to meet the needs of those around us.

\\\

In this case, the strength of your vertical relationship with God will give you the confidence and grace you need in order to serve effectively in your horizontal relationships with others. If Christ took on the form of a servant, and we are to be like Him, then our task is clear. The higher our worldly position, the lower we should bend to meet the needs of those around us. That is how we are to serve each other as a horizontal Jesus—on our knees with a towel and a basin.

How can you get on the path to greatness today? Get creative. You probably won't need to carry a basin and towel around your office or school. James 1:27 tells us, "Pure and undefiled religion in the sight of our God and Father is this: to visit orphans and widows in their distress, and to keep oneself unstained by the world." As you keep your eye out for opportunities to do the good works God has prepared for you, remember this: True religion serves others—especially those who aren't likely to pay you back.

10

FORGIVING
ONE ANOTHER

We have all seen dogs being walked on a leash. The dog is free to go a little distance but no farther. If it tries to bolt, it is yanked back and quickly reminded that its freedom of movement is limited.

Many people today go through life on a spiritual leash. The links in the chain include such things as anger, bitterness, resentment, wrath, and revenge. Together, these links create a chain of unforgiveness. Far too many of us are leashed by this powerful emotion. Maybe you know what I'm talking about as well. Perhaps unforgiveness has held you back from pursuing relationships, mending other ones, or deepening your intimacy with God. Unforgiveness is a nemesis that can own you for months, years, or even decades. One thing is for sure—breaking free from the chain of unforgiveness is no easy task.

Maybe you've seen the meme that says, "To error is human. To forgive…that ain't gonna happen." Many of us struggle with the willingness or the ability to forgive.

A counselor once told his client, "The next time you see the person who has hurt you, say, 'Happy New Year.'" The client was to wish his enemy happiness as a way of overcoming his unforgiveness.

The client wanted to comply with his counselor, so the next time he saw the man who had hurt him, he said, "I wish you a Happy New Year—but only one."

Some time ago, Lois and I took a much-anticipated trip to Hawaii. We needed a rest after several months of working through a busy schedule, so we were really looking forward to some peace and quiet. We couldn't wait to see the refreshing views and hear the calming sounds of the sea. I was scheduled to preach at a conference in Hawaii, so we maximized the opportunity by tagging on a few vacation days afterward. We needed it. When we boarded our flight, we were tired and worn out. But we were confident that once we got there, all would be well.

We were wrong.

A few minutes after we unpacked our bags, we discovered that the resort hotel where we were staying was having some...issues. It was undergoing a major renovation, and no one had bothered to let us know. Hammers banged and power saws screeched nonstop from early morning until late each evening. The noise drowned out the ocean waves and kept us from what we had come there to do—rest and recoup so we could move forward with strength.

To top it off, toward the end of this already chaotic trip, I wound up so sick that I had to be rushed to the hospital. I had never experienced that level of pain before. I remember sitting in the car on the frantic drive to the hospital, doubled over, thinking, "This isn't how Hawaii is supposed to be." It was awful. For a couple days I stayed in the hospital, which was almost as noisy as the hotel.

By the time Lois and I boarded the plane back to Dallas, we were more tired than when we had left.

> Sin always creates a mess. Forgiveness
> is how you remove yourself from it.

It's amazing what someone else's mess will do to you, isn't it? It can keep you from seeing the beauty around you and from getting what you need in order to move through life with strength. It's also amazing what your own mess can do.

Whether the mess is your own or someone else's, it keeps you from moving forward. It blocks your view and slows your progress. Like a crying baby on an airplane, it absorbs the energy and attention you had wanted to put elsewhere.

Sin always creates a mess. Maybe someone has sinned against you and you need to forgive them. Or maybe you have sinned and now struggle with guilt and shame. Perhaps you're struggling with "compounded sin"—your sinful reaction to other people's offenses against you. All of these create a mess. And mess has a way of preventing you from being all that you were created to be.

That's why forgiveness is so important. It's how you remove yourself from the mess all around you and in you.

Not only that, but forgiveness also impacts our vertical experience with God. God makes clear that the relational forgiveness we experience with Him is tied to our choice to forgive those who have offended us. Of all of the scriptural "one anothers" we are studying, our horizontal forgiveness is the most clearly connected to our vertical forgiveness from above.

Relational Forgiveness

Now, just to be clear, I am not talking about the forgiveness we receive from Christ's death on the cross, which gains us entrance into heaven. That is called judicial, or legal, forgiveness. Every person who is saved by coming to Jesus Christ for the forgiveness of their sins has experienced judicial forgiveness. That is the forgiveness for your offenses against a holy God. Judicial forgiveness is eternal, which is why as a Christian, you cannot lose your salvation. The judgment bar has declared you not guilty once and for all.

Actually, you are guilty. We all are. But we have been *declared* not guilty because of the work of Christ. Scripture calls that justification.

But justification (judicial forgiveness, or legal forgiveness) is not the only kind of forgiveness. The other kind is relational forgiveness. This has to do with our experiential fellowship with God and the closeness we sense with Him. The best illustration of this occurs in marriage. Many people are legally married, yet they are miserable due to a break in their relationship. The same is true in our relationship with God. We can be saved and on our way to heaven yet also be unhappy and defeated because our fellowship with the Lord is not intact. When this happens, the problem is often unforgiveness.

Bearing with One Another

Paul describes this concept of forgiveness.

> So, as those who have been chosen of God, holy and beloved, put on a heart of compassion, kindness, humility, gentleness and patience; bearing with one another, and *forgiving each other*, whoever has a complaint against anyone; just as the Lord forgave you, so also should you (Colossians 3:12-13).

Before we go further, let me first clarify what forgiveness *doesn't* mean—it doesn't mean approving, excusing, or justifying the wrong committed against you. Nor does it mean pretending that you haven't been hurt. Likewise, it doesn't mean that reconciliation has occurred or ever will.

Forgiveness is a decision, not an emotion.

Biblical forgiveness is the decision to no longer credit an offense against an offender. It involves releasing someone from a debt they owe and the blame they deserve. And it includes choosing not to take vengeance.

Keep in mind that forgiveness is a decision. It is not primarily an emotion. It's not about how you are feeling, but about your choice to no longer credit an offense or blame against an offender. The heart of forgiveness is wiping a trespass off the offender's record (Romans 4:8).

Sometimes, the offender you need to forgive is you.

The best biblical description of forgiveness is found in 1 Corinthians 13:5, where we read that love "keeps no record of wrongs" (NIV). That doesn't mean love justifies the wrong—that isn't loving others; it's enabling them. Neither does it mean that love ignores the wrong, excuses it, or pretends that it didn't happen. Like an alcoholic's spouse continuing to clean up the mess from the previous night's disaster, this only provides the opportunity for the offense (the sin) to continue. And that's not love either.

Love means not keeping a record of wrongs. This is similar to how God forgives us. He doesn't forget the sin, but He no longer holds the offense against our account. We are not indebted to Him to pay off something that we are unable to pay.

We must decide—will we push the delete button on a wrong done?

Everyone has spent plenty of time on both sides of the forgiveness equation. We have all needed to be forgiven, and we have all needed to forgive. Forgiveness is the quintessential issue of human relationships. We must decide—will we push the delete button on a wrong done? No other choice raises such conflicting emotions in us. And no other issue can help or hinder our relationships with ourselves, with others, and with God. In fact, our choice to forgive even affects what God is willing to do in and through our lives.

Forgiveness Moves Mountains

How do you climb a mountain? One step at a time. But God's plan for you doesn't just involve scaling mountains one step at a time. He actually wants you to move them.

Maybe you are facing an impossible situation in your life right now—a circumstance that seems to be insurmountable. You can't figure out how to fix it or change it, and as far as you can see, there doesn't seem to be any light at the end of the tunnel. You can't climb over it. You can't dig through it. And you feel stuck at the base of it.

There may be a reason why you are not overcoming the mountain you are facing right now. Often, that reason is unforgiveness.

Your insurmountable situation may be professional or relational. It could be a health issue or a character defect you are trying to overcome. Whatever it is, it seems too high, too wide, too thick, and too steep to overcome. The Bible often uses mountains to represent situations you cannot solve, struggles you cannot win, or pain you cannot dull (Zechariah 4:7). There may be a reason why you are not overcoming the mountain you are facing right now. Often, that reason is unforgiveness.

When Jesus taught us how to pray, He said that if we do not doubt in our hearts but believe that what we say is going to happen, we can move a mountain (Mark 11:22-24). Then He gave us a clue as to why our prayers may not be moving much of anything at all.

> Whenever you stand praying, forgive, if you have anything against anyone, so that your Father who is in heaven will also forgive you your transgressions. But if you do not forgive, neither will your Father who is in heaven forgive your transgressions (verses 25-26).

If God is to empower you to move the mountains you are facing today, you must forgive. Moving mountains is conditioned on the purity of your relationship with God. And the purity of that relationship hinges on forgiveness. If there is anything that blocks the flow of God's power in your life more than all else, it is unforgiveness.

Here's the point. You have a mountain in your life that you want God to supernaturally move. And He will, but there's a condition. Jesus tells us that the refusal to forgive another person will block your experience of God's relational forgiveness of you.

If your fellowship with God is hindered because you are refusing to forgive someone else, then He is not hearing or answering your prayers the way He could if that relational channel was open. This is because it takes faith to move a mountain. And it takes faith to forgive—faith that God is sovereign, faith that He has a plan for allowing what He does, and faith that He will use whatever happens for your good. When you don't forgive, you are telling God that you don't believe He has a purpose for the pain. You are telling God that you don't trust Him.

"Forgiveness" is a beautiful word when someone is giving it to you. It's a much more challenging word when you have to give it to someone else. But God has forgiven us of a debt we could never pay, and that motivates us to forgive others of their smaller debts against us (see Matthew 18:23-35).

You never want to burn a bridge over which you yourself will have to cross. You don't want to live in a relationally unforgiven state with a holy God because you refuse to forgive those who have offended you. Jesus taught us to pray, "Forgive us our debts, as we also have forgiven our debtors" (Matthew 6:12). In order to receive relational forgiveness and exercise a faith that can move mountains, you will need to forgive.

> A man's discretion makes him slow to anger,
> And it is his glory to overlook a transgression.
> Proverbs 19:11

Unilateral Forgiveness

Let's consider two types of forgiveness so you can apply them to your situation. The first type is *unilateral forgiveness*, which involves forgiving someone who has not asked you to forgive them. They may not know they have offended you, they may have moved away, or they may no longer be alive. Unilateral forgiveness means forgiving others even if they haven't apologized or repented. Steven offered this type of forgiveness when he was being stoned to death. "He cried out with a loud voice, 'Lord, do not hold this sin against them!'" (Acts 7:60). Jesus did the same on the cross when He said, "Father, forgive them; for they do not know what they are doing" (Luke 23:34).

One day, a man who was driving without insurance ran into my car. I had two options. I could have my insurance company pay for the repairs, or I could drive around with a dent in my car. I had the car fixed, but imagine for a moment what could have happened if I hadn't. Every time I walked out to get into my car, I would see the dent, think about the other driver, remember what he did, and get angry all over again.

<hr/>

Unilateral forgiveness can free you
from troubling emotions.

<hr/>

Unfortunately a lot of people today are living with dents in their souls. The dents were caused by people who offended them in some way but never apologized or tried to repair what was broken. Maybe you have a dent like this as well, and every time you see that dent, you feel angry or bitter toward the person who caused it. Maybe you're filled with regret.

Unilateral forgiveness can free you from those troubling emotions. And it's based on God's forgiveness for you. "God demonstrates His own love toward us, in that while we were yet sinners, Christ died for us" (Romans 5:8).

Transactional Forgiveness

The second type of forgiveness is called *transactional forgiveness*. When someone who has sinned against you confesses and repents, and you respond with forgiveness, a transaction has occurred. It's a two-way exchange. The offender has demonstrated that they are indeed sorry for what they have done. When you offer transactional forgiveness, you open the door for the possibility of reconciliation.

The process of transactional forgiveness can be tricky because you don't always know the offender's motive for apologizing. The offender may truly be repentant. On the other hand, the person may be confessing simply because they got caught and are trying to avoid the consequences.

Sometimes people offer forgiveness and reconciliation because the other person said he or she was sorry and seemed repentant, but before long, it becomes clear that there was not a "change of mind" about the offense. So the offense occurs again and again—each time with yet another apology. It's important to bear in mind that people will often say they are sorry simply because they got caught and they are only trying to lessen or avoid the consequences.

So it's important to note that there are two components to transactional forgiveness—forgiveness and reconciliation. Always try to offer forgiveness as soon as you can. But offer reconciliation only after offenders demonstrate true repentance and take steps to stop their inappropriate behavior.

When you offer transactional forgiveness, you open the door for the possibility of reconciliation.

So when you are offering transactional forgiveness, you forgive right away. But before you reconcile the relationship, you must test the fruit of repentance. This is similar to what Joseph did when his brothers asked him to forgive them in Egypt. In Genesis 42:15-16, we read that Joseph actually told his brothers he was testing them to find out whether they were telling the truth. At the time, his brothers didn't know this was the brother they had lied about and sold into slavery. But Joseph remembered what they had done to him 22 years earlier, and because of that, he tested their heart and character to see whether they had changed or remained the same.

Saying "I'm sorry" is one thing. But if the apology is not accompanied by the fruits of repentance, it might actually mean "I'm sorry I got caught."

True repentance leads to life. That's what Peter experienced after he denied Jesus three times and then went out and wept. Jesus knew Peter's repentance was genuine, and He restored Peter to a position of service. On the other hand, remorse leads to death. The Bible says that after Judas betrayed the Lord, he was "seized with remorse" (Matthew 27:3 NIV)—and then went out and hanged himself. In 2 Corinthians 7:10-11, Paul talks about the difference between godly sorrow (producing repentance without regret, which leads to salvation) and worldly sorrow (which produces death).

When someone seeks transactional forgiveness and then wants to reconcile with you, take time to weigh their words and actions. Confirm that they are offering true repentance and not just remorse before you restore the relationship. It is important to see that they have truly turned from the sin they committed against you.

Forgiveness and Pain

At our radio broadcast ministry, The Urban Alternative, we have carefully chosen a tagline that reflects our mission and vision for the ministry—"Teaching truth and transforming lives." God has His own tagline of sorts, and He put it at the end of Jesus's model prayer in Matthew 6:9-13. This tagline isn't often quoted in the Lord's Prayer or included in teachings about a healthy prayer life. In fact, we sometimes bristle when we hear it because it seems harsh. But if we want to hear from God and see Him show up in our lives, we cannot ignore it.

God's tagline reads, "For if you forgive others for their transgressions, your heavenly Father will also forgive you. But if you do not forgive others, then your Father will not forgive your transgressions."

In order for each of us to be forgiven (relationally by God), we must also forgive (relationally each other.)

<hr>

When you forgive, you cross over
into the supernatural realm.

<hr>

Many of us have restricted our fellowship with the Father because we are unwilling to forgive one another. If you refuse to forgive someone, God makes it clear that you and He are not on the same page. In fact, you have blocked God's operational flow in your life. No matter how many prayers you pray, how many Bible verses you read, how many church services you attend, and the like, if you choose not to forgive others as a horizontal expression of Christ's love, you have broken your vertical fellowship with God. I didn't make that up. God did.

If you want forgiveness, be willing to give it. "For judgment will be merciless to one who has shown no mercy; mercy triumphs over judgment" (James 2:13).

When you forgive, you cross over into the supernatural realm. As difficult as it may be, you increase your relational bond with the Holy Spirit (Ephesians 4:30-32), and you open the door for God to do the amazing things He desires to do in your life—including helping you to forget the pain of the offense.

When Joseph was sold as a slave by his brothers, taken away as a captive, thrown in jail on false charges, and forgotten there, he had no doubt accumulated a lot of pain to carry around with him. Yet as we see in the book of Genesis, Joseph chose to forgive. As a result, the pain dissipated. I know this because of the name Joseph chose for one of his sons. He named him Manasseh, which sounds like the Hebrew word for "forget." When you choose to forgive, God will also help you to forget. You may never forget what happened—Joseph didn't either. But you will be freed from the debilitating pain and empowered to move forward into God's destiny for you.

11

Admonishing
One Another

Several years ago I had to climb up on the roof of my house. I pulled out the ladder, leaned it against the gutter, and began to climb.

The ladder was easily tall enough to get me from the ground to the roof. It was well built and more than strong enough to support me. But the higher I climbed up the ladder, the shakier it became. As I slowed my steps, I realized the ladder was about to fall. I quickly jumped off—and twisted my ankle as I hit the ground.

The problem wasn't the ladder. The problem was, the stable ladder was resting on unstable ground. I had set it on ground that was somewhat soft, and as I climbed, the ladder began to shift and move in the ground. So even though the rungs were sound, without the right foundation, they became useless.

Many people today are trying to climb from where they are to where they want to go, only to find out along the way that the ladder they are climbing is not keeping them up. Twelve-step programs designed to take people from problems to victory can be helpful, but they often don't produce what they promised they could. Support groups don't always produce lasting effects. Psychologists and counselors can also be helpful, but if these ladders aren't resting on a solid foundation, people's problems are likely to compound.

And even if you are not personally at the point of seeing a counselor, attending a 12-step program, or going to a support group, life in general produces challenges and shifts that can leave you up one day and down the next. Sometimes you can even be up one hour and down the next. Such is life. Circumstances change, and we return to our old habits—overspending, overeating, gossiping, or looking to other unhealthy distractions to help us cope.

How can we fortify our foundations and empower each other to continue climbing the ladder of destiny that Christ Jesus has in store for each of us? By creating a community of believers who lovingly admonish one another. If I had invited someone to join me that day as I climbed toward the roof of my house, that person could have pointed out that the ladder was on unstable ground. I would have moved it, finished my task, and saved myself the pain of a twisted ankle. The apostle Paul expected believers to admonish each other.

> Now may the God of hope fill you with all joy and peace in believing, so that you will abound in hope by the power of the Holy Spirit.
>
> And concerning you, my brethren, I myself also am convinced that you yourselves are full of goodness, filled with all knowledge and able also to *admonish one another* (Romans 15:13-14).

The Greek word translated "admonish" is *noutheteo* (counsel, advise, steer, or warn). Paul uses the same word when he writes, "Let the word of Christ richly dwell within you, with all wisdom teaching and *admonishing* one another with psalms and hymns and spiritual songs, singing with thankfulness in your hearts to God" (Colossians 3:16). When you and I read that we are to admonish one another, we are being encouraged to counsel, guide, steer, and direct the people in our sphere of influence. The verse isn't saying that we are to be professional psychologists or analysts, but that as Christians in the family of God, we are to provide biblical, spiritual counsel to one another. We are to provide instruction, exhortation, or even warning, depending on the situation, to those who need direction in their lives.

Noutheteo specifically has to do with providing corrective or intentional guidance in order to prevent something that could go wrong or to direct toward something that would be right. It includes guidance away from choices that are sinful as well as those that might simply be unwise. To admonish is to counsel, whether formally or informally.

///

As members of Christ's body, we are called
to invest in one another's spiritual growth.

\\

Paul identifies the goal of our admonishment. "We proclaim Him, *admonishing* every man and teaching every man with all wisdom, so that we may present every man complete in Christ" (Colossians 1:28). The goal of admonishing one another is spiritual maturity. Our aim is to help every man and woman to be complete in Christ, mature and whole. We do this by helping each other place our ladders on the solid foundation of biblical truth and wisdom.

Admonishment isn't running around pointing fingers and making people look bad. Rather, it is constructive counsel, guidance, and teaching. These passages and others reveal that as members of Christ's body, we are called to enhance, develop, and invest in one another's spiritual growth. That's not simply the pastor's job or the Sunday school teacher's job. That responsibility rests on all of our shoulders. We are to be a horizontal Jesus to one another, offering wisdom, insight, and counsel where needed.

When we admonish one another in love, we make ourselves candidates for experiencing a greater level of God's mercy in our own lives. Our vertical experience with God is enhanced by caring horizontal relationships.

What Is a Mature Believer?

If our goal is to help each other become mature Christians, how do we measure that goal? What does a mature Christian look, act, and sound like?

Mature believers consistently make decisions based on a biblical worldview. They seek to live life under God and His comprehensive rule over everything. Maturity is about consistency, not perfection. It can be measured in the many small decisions we make according to God's perspective, not man's limited and skewed point of view.

As followers and disciples of Christ, our goal is to reflect a divine viewpoint in all we do or say and to empower others to do the same. When this freely and repeatedly occurs in our lives, we are living in maturity. To achieve that, as Paul reminds us, we need to be admonishing one another. Spiritual growth doesn't happen in a vacuum, and it doesn't happen simply because we clock in and out of church on Sunday mornings and Wednesday nights. Spiritual growth is an ongoing process of development that includes aligning our minds to God's perspective.

Full of Goodness

In the passages we are studying in this chapter, Paul gives us two qualifications for counseling and advising one another. We see the first one in Romans 15:14, where we read, "And concerning you, my brethren, I myself also am convinced that you yourselves are *full of goodness*." In order to admonish others effectively, we need to be full of goodness. We are to have an upright lifestyle. We are to be godly, learning how to please the Lord and align ourselves under Him so we can help other people do the same.

This doesn't mean we will be perfect. None of us is perfect (Ecclesiastes 7:20; Romans 3:10). Rather, it means we are consistently seeking to move toward maturity. We are committed to honoring God with our words, heart, and actions.

If the Bible doesn't make a call on something, we shouldn't judge someone else for their viewpoint.

This brings us to a discussion on a very important topic in the Christian church—judging. Jesus warned us, "Do not judge so that you will not be judged" (Matthew 7:1). We've seen that we are not to judge each other's preferences (Romans 14:1). We have no right to do that. A preference is an opinion—something personal to you that the Bible does not specifically require or condemn. If the Bible doesn't make a call on something, we shouldn't judge someone else for their viewpoint.

Yet the Bible also tells us that we *are* to judge. A few verses after Jesus tells us not to judge, He says, "Beware of the false prophets, who come to you in sheep's clothing, but inwardly are ravenous wolves. You will know them by their fruits" (Matthew 7:15-16). Obviously, to know people by their fruits, you have to make a judgment call on what they are doing.

So first we are told not to judge, and then we are told to judge. When the Bible does not speak clearly on a certain issue, we are not to judge people's opinions on the matter. But we are to judge whether people's lives clearly conflict with biblical truth.

Spiritual maturity gives us the ability to judge between right and wrong. "Solid food is for the mature, who because of practice have their senses trained to discern good and evil" (Hebrews 5:14). And if you think that only applies to the good and evil in your own life, look at Paul's direct condemnation of other believers who failed to make proper judgment, and notice that he offered his own personal judgment in response.

> It is actually reported that there is immorality among you, and immorality of such a kind as does not exist even among the Gentiles, that someone has his father's wife. You have become arrogant and have not mourned instead, so that the one who had done this deed would be removed from your midst.
>
> For I, on my part, though absent in body but present in spirit, have already judged him who has so committed this, as though I were present. In the name of our Lord Jesus, when you are assembled, and I with you in spirit, with the power of our Lord Jesus, I have decided to deliver such a one to Satan for the destruction of his flesh, so that his spirit may be saved in the day of the Lord Jesus (1 Corinthians 5:1-5).

Paul clearly tells the believers in Corinth that he is disappointed that they did not judge their brother, and then he goes on to judge that person himself. In the next chapter, Paul writes, "Do you not know that we will judge angels? How much more matters of this life?"

(1 Corinthians 6:3). The apostle Peter agrees—"For it is time for judgment to begin with the household of God" (1 Peter 4:17).

Jesus is not saying we should never judge. He is teaching us how to make good judgments.

So which is it? Are we not to judge one another, or are we to judge? A deeper look at Matthew 7:1 reveals the answer. When we quote, "Do not judge so that you will not be judged," we often fail to include the next sentence: "For in the way you judge, you will be judged; and by your standard of measure, it will be measured to you." By adding the context we see that Jesus is not saying we should never judge. He is teaching us how to make good judgments. He goes on to give a concrete example that clarifies this even more.

> Why do you look at the speck that is in your brothers' eye, but do not notice the log that is in your own eye? Or how can you say to your brother, "Let me take the speck out of your eye," and behold, the log is in your own eye? You hypocrite, first take the log out of your own eye, and then you will see clearly to take the speck out of your brother's eye (Matthew 7:3-5).

Jesus finishes the illustration by saying, "And then you will see clearly to take the speck out of your brother's eye." He doesn't tell us to focus only on what is wrong in our own lives. Rather, he tells us to start there. His point is, if you are going to judge someone (based on biblical truth and not preference), make sure you are qualified. What qualifies you to make that judgment? It's your own level of alignment under God.

This is especially important when you are judging someone else on an issue you are dealing with in your own life. Sawdust and logs are made from the same material—wood. Therefore you disqualify yourself as a judge when you are doing the same thing the other person is doing. That is called being a hypocrite.

Paul tells us we are to be full of goodness first, which then qualifies us to judge, admonish, and counsel. We are to provide insight and direction to others in those areas where the Lord has already brought us through and provided us with the victory in Christ Jesus.

Would you go to a blind ophthalmologist? Neither would I. The starting point for encouraging and counseling someone else is personal excellence and goodness in that area ourselves. If we're not there yet, we need to leave that one alone and focus on our own spiritual growth in that arena. Have you ever noticed that people like to judge in areas where they are the weakest? Somehow it makes us feel better to point out that someone else is failing in the same way we are. Yet that is exactly where God instructs us *not* to judge because we aren't in a position to help anybody.

This is similar to what we are instructed to do on the airplane if we were to ever lose oxygen. The steward always gives the instruction that we are to put on our own oxygen masks first before we help anyone sitting next to us. If you can't breathe yourself, you can't help someone else either. Take care of your own need and lack before you seek to admonish and guide someone else in that same area.

Filled with Knowledge

The first qualification for admonishing someone else is that you are full of goodness in the area where you are seeking to guide and counsel them. The second qualification is that you are filled with all knowledge. Paul writes, "And concerning you, my brethren, I myself also am convinced that you yourselves are full of goodness, *filled with all knowledge.*" The first qualification involves your personal lifestyle in the area you're addressing. The second qualification involves the information you're delivering. Do you have God's perspective on the matter? Are you relaying divine knowledge or merely spreading worldly wisdom? We've seen Paul's exhortation to "let the word of Christ richly dwell within you, with all wisdom teaching and admonishing one another" (Colossians 3:16).

> God's Word coupled with a good life provide
> the solid foundation where people can plant their
> ladders and climb toward their God-given destiny.

The Holy Spirit uses God's truth in each of our lives, so when we give counsel and advice that is based merely on human opinion, we are not offering anything the Spirit uses to transform lives. That's why the "word of Christ" must first dwell within us before we are able to teach and admonish one another. Otherwise we are wasting our time by merely sharing our opinions.

The Holy Spirit is released to do His work when our counsel flows from a good life and the good Word. When the life and Word match, the Holy Spirit uses our counsel and intervenes to deliver others. But if our lives and the Word are not matching, there will be reduced power. God's Word coupled with a good life provide the solid foundation where people can plant their ladders and climb toward their God-given destiny.

Checking Your Motivation

Being full of goodness and the Word isn't always easy. We must be motivated by authentic care and love, and we must exert some effort. That's what Paul modeled for the elders from Ephesus.

> Be on the alert, remembering that night and day for a period of three years I did not cease to admonish each one with tears. And now I commend you to God and to the word of His grace, which is able to build you up and to give you the inheritance among all those who are sanctified (Acts 20:31-32).

If you don't have a heartfelt concern for the person you are guiding and correcting, your counsel will sound as if you're saying, "I told you so!"

Paul's admonishment to these Ephesians came with tears. Tears indicate an authentic and genuine care for the well-being of the person you are trying to help. We are to be "speaking the truth in love" (Ephesians 4:15). But if you don't have a heartfelt concern for the person you are guiding and correcting, your counsel will sound as if you're saying, "I told you so!"

When we admonish others, we're not simply fulfilling an obligation. If we're merely checking an item off our to-do list, we'll never have the commitment we need to remain consistent. Paul reminded the Ephesians that he admonished them "night and day for a period of three years," demonstrating his heartfelt concern. He was willing to hang in there.

Consider a master surgeon. I'll tell you one thing a good surgeon is not—he's not a slasher. He's not trying to hurt you as he cuts you. In fact, he's trying to make the cut so minimal that when you heal later, the scar will hardly be noticeable. Yes, you may hurt and bleed when he operates, but he works with the utmost tenderness, precision, and care to provide you with the greatest opportunity for healing.

That's how we are to admonish one another—not with a vicious tongue or heart, but in true love, placing the highest value on others' well-being. Paul writes in 1 Corinthians 4:14, "I do not write these things to shame you, but to admonish you as my beloved children." The intent is never to shame, embarrass, or harass. The intent of admonishment is always the betterment of another through gentle and corrective guidance.

> You don't need a bullhorn to be a biblical counselor—you need love.

Here is one way to test whether your motives are pure. Do you tell others about the situation before you tell that person? Do you tell others what happened afterward? If so, you can know right then and there that your motives are not pure. We are to go to the person first and in private when correcting or guiding him. It doesn't need to be broadcast on social media or in texts and conversations. You don't need a bullhorn to be a biblical counselor—you need love.

Some people in your church, circle, class, or small group are making unwise choices—even sinful ones. Sermons aren't always going to reach them. Neither will nice songs sung on Sunday morning. What they need is the Holy Spirit showing up in their lives through someone who cares enough to offer heartfelt counsel based on the Word of God. They need a friend. A friend is someone who gets in your way when you are on your way down. That's a true friend. A friend is not someone who rats on you publicly, but someone who tries to restore you privately.

I'll share a personal example. It's not one of my proudest moments, but I hope it will make the point. When I was still living at home as a teenager in Baltimore, my brother Bo did something wrong. I can't remember what it was now, but I do remember going straight to my dad and ratting on Bo. My father replied, "Send Bo to the basement," which I gladly did.

After my dad disciplined Bo in the basement, he told Bo to send me down as well. I walked down to the basement unsure why my dad wanted to see me. But it didn't take long for him to let me know. He had called me to the basement for my punishment as well!

When I asked my dad why I was getting punished, he told me I missed an opportunity to correct Bo's behavior when I saw him doing something wrong. Rather than admonishing and restoring my brother, I chose to tattle on him instead. I could have delivered him from his punishment, but instead I delivered him *to* his punishment. My dad clearly saw what I was doing. My motive was to get my brother in trouble, and that deserved punishment. Friend, motivation matters. Why we do what we do matters at least as much as what we do.

As you and I seek to be obedient to God in this sensitive area of admonition, let's begin by recognizing each other as brothers and sisters in Christ, dearly loved by the Lord. Then let's seek to restore each other through admonition and not to take each other down. View admonishment through the lens of counsel and couple it with a right heart, right life, and God's Word. Then you will fulfill your call to live as a horizontal Jesus to those around you.

12

RESTORING ONE ANOTHER

Hospitals exist because people get sick. When people need their health restored, hospitals are there to combat the illness and facilitate healing. At a hospital, doctors and nurses do for others what people cannot do for themselves. They make people well again.

The church, the body of Christ, is God's hospital. One of the primary reasons the church exists is to be a community where people's spiritual lives can be restored. They certainly can't restore themselves. People desperately need help—something has gone wrong in their lives, and the church is there to facilitate healing. As members of God's family, we join together to offer the hope of healing by God's grace.

As a reminder, if you want the deepest experience of your vertical relationship with God, check your horizontal relationships with the family of God. You are not an only child in God's family. People in healthy families always share responsibilities. The church is a spiritual family of believers, so our relationship with God correlates in various ways with our relationships with one another. If you ignore the "one anothers" in the Bible, you won't receive everything God wants to give you.

Imagine a child who ignores his siblings but wants to be close to his father. His relationship with his dad will be hindered by his disconnection from his brothers and sisters. God wants you to be a dynamic part of a local body of believers so you can position yourself to experience more of Him as you engage with others. That includes living out the "one another" we are looking at together in this chapter, which is to *restore one another*. The church family is to be a place where those who are spiritually weak or sick can find help, hope, healing, and restoration in Christ's name.

> Brethren, even if anyone is caught in any trespass, you who are spiritual, restore such a one in a spirit of gentleness; each one looking to yourself, so that you too will not be tempted. Bear one another's burdens, and thereby fulfill the law of Christ (Galatians 6:1-2).

The Greek word translated "restore" means to mend something that has been broken. It sometimes referred to mending a broken bone. The bone would be reset so it could grow back together and be restored to its original function. Or if a fisherman tore his net, he would restore it by mending the place that was torn.

The process of restoration doesn't always feel good at the time, but it should produce a good result. Restoration is like braces on crooked teeth. They might hurt when the orthodontist tightens them or as the teeth shift into place. But ultimately, the restored smile will be worth the pain.

Before people can be restored, they must acknowledge that something has been broken or torn and needs to be mended. In the same way that people go to the hospital to regain their health, people who come to church ought to be able to find restoration for their broken lives. God uses us to mend one another according to our original design as much as possible.

Getting Caught

Why is restoration needed? As we see from the text, oftentimes someone is stuck in a sin and can't get out. Paul wrote, "If anyone is caught in a trespass..." referring to a sin they cannot overcome. They may be caught in an addiction. It could be obvious, like an addiction to alcohol, drugs, pornography, or illicit sex. Or it could be hidden, like an addiction to negative self-talk. They may be addicted to gossip, racism, overspending, or overworking. Whenever people's dependence on an activity begins to control their lives, they are caught in an addiction. They have begun serving an idol. They have been broken or torn and need to be restored by God.

Whatever the case, Paul is referring to something that has bound them and will not let them go. They are hostage to it. That's what Paul means by being "caught" in a trespass. They want to get free, but they can't. Like a fish on a well-set hook, they can wiggle all they want, but they can't get loose.

Sin has a way of doing that. At first, you may be able to break free, but over time, the sin develops into an addiction—the hook is in so deep that you are unable to find freedom on your own. In fact, fish hooks have barbs so that the more the fish wiggles, trying to free itself, the deeper the hook is set.

This is the scenario Paul is describing when he refers to someone being "caught" in a trespass. He isn't referring to someone who doesn't want to be free. Restoration comes to the person who desires healing, just as patients in a hospital want to get well. A sick person who chooses not to go to the hospital may want healing but won't take the necessary action steps. They still think they can beat it on their own.

Some people in the church are so deep in their sin that no matter what they do, they are unable to overcome it. Have you ever seen a dog tethered to a pole, circling the pole again and again until the leash is mostly wrapped around the pole and the dog is hardly able to move? In the same way, these people want to be free but are no longer able to find their way to freedom on their own. When this happens, we in the body of Christ are called to restore these people—to offer the guidance, help, correction, and patience they need to find healing and hope.

"You Who Are Spiritual"

Notice Paul's careful qualification when he directs us to this high calling of restoration. He says, "You who are spiritual..." The business of restoration in the church is as serious as the business of restoring health in a hospital. If it is not done right, even greater bondage can occur. What might happen if a person needed surgery but chose a practitioner without a medical degree and without any legitimate experience? The patient would undoubtedly suffer even more.

Problems in the physical world have spiritual roots, and those who suffer need spiritual deliverance and restoration.

Restoration must happen in the body of Christ, but Paul states clearly that it must be done by the qualified—those who are spiritual. If it is not done "in a spirit of gentleness" and wisdom, the one who is seeking to restore can cause more harm than good and also be pulled into the bondage themselves.

Some believers don't get delivered from sin because they seek the help of those who cannot restore them—people who are not spiritual themselves. Problems in the physical world have spiritual roots, and those who suffer need spiritual deliverance and restoration. That's why Paul says the ones who are spiritual need to do the restoring. When you go to a doctor, you want that doctor to know what he's doing. You don't want just anyone showing up saying, "I think I can help you." When you are sick and in pain, you need a doctor who knows how to treat you and deliver you from your illness.

The same is true spiritually. But far too often, believers offer unbiblical advice to one another—advice that is not founded on the Word of God and lived out in obedience. The advice might sound good, but in the end, restoration does not occur.

What does it mean to be spiritual? Being spiritual means you have sought God's assessment of the problem. God has both defined the problem and given the solution. That's what it means to be spiritual—to have the Holy Spirit illuminate your mind with the truth of God's Word. A spiritual approach to life's addictions and sins is needed because the outward symptoms aren't typically the underlying cause.

When you go to the doctor complaining of a physical pain, he doesn't just hand you some aspirins. Rather, he probes deeper. He may request blood work or a CAT scan. The doctor wants to know the true cause so he can prescribe the true cure. Likewise, you can't treat something spiritually simply by looking at the symptoms. You must discover the spiritual cause and treat it spiritually in order to restore someone.

The Grace of Gentleness

Being spiritual has nothing to do with the degrees on your wall or how much education you have. A high school dropout can be more spiritual that a person with a master's degree in theology. In fact, I know some people who have seminary degrees but who are still not spiritual.

And spirituality has nothing to do with how old you are. A person could be 90 years old but have lived carnally for those 90 years. Neither does being spiritual have to do with how many Bible verses you have memorized, how many church services you have attended, or how much money you give. Those can be helpful activities, but you can do all of them and still not be spiritual.

Spirituality has to do with the means you use to view life. Spiritual people look at life with God's perspective and through the lens of His Word. They know God's Word and apply it to their lives. Any Bible-centered body of believers should be marked by their ability to restore those who have fallen or are on a wrong path. When judgment and shunning outweigh restoration and reconciliation, a church is not living according to God's Word, which tells us that we are to be spiritual enough to gently restore one another.

When our kids were younger, we took them to a Christian family camp every year. Each time we went, I took them down to the dock to fish. Now, the whole point was to enjoy the experience. We had no intention of keeping, cleaning, or eating the fish. So each time we caught a fish, my job was to gently remove the hook and cradle the fish underwater until it swam away. When Paul talks about us restoring one another in a spirit of gentleness, he is referring to how we go about removing the obstacles or sins in other people's lives.

When I held on to that fish to remove the hook, I didn't squeeze it so hard that it felt excruciating pain. Neither did I grab the line and yank the hook from its mouth. My intention in removing the hook was to restore the fish to its original habitat in good condition. I gently held the fish and carefully rotated the hook until it came free.

When we have an opportunity to restore someone's broken relationship with Jesus Christ by removing a hindrance or sin in their lives, we are to use a spirit of gentleness and kindness. That way, when the person is restored, they are not encumbered with ongoing pain and emotional scars. Unfortunately, far too many believers today seem to berate rather than restore each other. They are quick to point fingers but slow to promote healing. Evidently, even when Paul wrote his letter to the Galatians, people were beating up each other with the Bible rather than restoring each other. We read, "The whole Law is fulfilled in one word, in the statement, 'You shall love your neighbor as yourself.' But if you bite and devour one another, take care that you are not consumed by one another" (Galatians 5:14-15).

Paul was warning them that if they move away from the law of love and turn instead to backbiting, criticizing, hurting, and destroying reputations, ultimately they will be consumed by one another. This is a "one another" that we don't want to experience in our churches and relationships today! That's not spiritual restoration— that's cannibalism!

Restoration occurs when God's people look beyond the symptoms to what God says. It happens when God's people address the source of the sin and help carry the burden that weighs someone down.

Bear One Another's Burdens...

You'll notice that Paul says we are to "bear one another's burdens" (Galatians 6:2). A burden is not necessarily a sin. A burden is a weight that is too heavy for someone to handle alone. Thus restoration involves more than just returning people to health and healing when they have been caught in sin. It also involves helping people to stand straight again after they have been burdened by life's trials and tribulations. They could be weighed down by issues with a child. Or they might be stumbling under a burden of poor health, finances, or work.

When our nation sank into the Great Recession of 2008 and 2009, many people lost work through no fault of their own. Due to the financial difficulties, many of those people also experienced strains in their family relationships and in their health. These are burdens that we are called to bear with one another.

God says we are to be each other's spotters.

I occasionally go to the gym to lift weights. I have a spotter who stands above me as I'm lifting in case the weight becomes too heavy for me to bear on my own. When that happens, the spotter intervenes to lift the burden from me. Similarly, when life gets too heavy for someone to lift on their own, God says we are to be each other's spotters. We are to be that person who comes alongside and lifts the weight, putting it back on the rack.

When we bear one another's burdens, Paul says we "fulfill the law of Christ." What is the law of Christ? The law of Christ is the law of love. It is the law we looked at in chapters 1 and 2. When we are fulfilling this law, we are truly living as a horizontal Jesus to one another. The apostle John writes, "Beloved, if God so loved us, we also ought to love one another" (1 John 4:11). Jesus said, "A new commandment I give to you, that you love one another, even as I have loved you, that you also love one another. By this all men will know that you are My disciples, if you have love for one another" (John 13:34-35).

When we bear one another's burdens and restore one another, we are loving one another. We are being a horizontal Jesus to one another. We are declaring to the world that we are Christ's disciples. In light of this truth, restoration is no small thing. Bearing each other's burdens is no small thing. In fact, it is the very thing that brings God glory and advances His kingdom on earth.

Have you seen a vehicle that was smashed so badly that the driver couldn't get out? If the first responders can't get the driver out, they call for the jaws of life—a tool they use to pry open the mangled car so they can gently lift the person out. In the same way, when people are caught in a trespass, we can come alongside them in the power of the Spirit, prying open the wreckage that has pinned them down. With a spirit of gentleness, we can lift them out and restore them on their way.

...But Don't Carry Their Load

When we restore others to spiritual health and help deliver them from their bondage, we need to keep something in mind. We must be careful to avoid *enabling* them. When you enable people in this sense, you do them more harm than good.

When we restore others, we bear their burdens long enough for them to heal and learn to walk again.

Perhaps you've experienced this. Someone is low on funds, and you lend them money. A week or a month later, they are back—not to repay you, but to ask for more money. They have a financial burden, and you want to help them bear that burden. But they must also acknowledge their own role in the process and fulfill it. Paul addressed this when he wrote, "Each one will bear his own load" (Galatians 6:5).

When we restore others, we bear their burdens long enough for them to heal and learn to walk again. As they regain their strength, we gradually, gently, and lovingly withdraw the support they needed when they were caught in debilitating sin. As their spiritual muscles develop, we transfer their belongings back to them so they can continue on their way. People are fully restored when they are standing straight and tall, bearing their own load, and walking freely again on the path to their own personal destiny.

But what happens if we continue to carry their load? They will never be fully restored. They won't develop the strength they need to bear their own load. They'll always be overly dependent on us. In fact, they will take advantage of the situation and continue to indulge in their sin, knowing we'll be there to clean up the mess.

And what happens to us if we continue to carry others' loads? In a fallen world with plenty of people caught in trespasses, we will get used up. People will find out they can turn to you, and before you know it, you will be maxed out.

Through the Spirit and in a spirit of gentleness,
we empower people to carry their own load.

When you restore someone, you are not called to take on their responsibilities. We do not deliver people from their responsibilities—we restore them into the freedom to fulfill their responsibilities. Through the Spirit and in a spirit of gentleness, we empower people to carry their own load.

You are to bear a burden but not carry a load. There is a difference. A load is smaller than a burden—it is something the person can handle. It is a responsibility the person must accept or an action they must take to put themselves on the path to freedom. We are to help those in need, but we are not to help them irresponsibly. Scripture says that if a man does not work, he ought not to eat (2 Thessalonians 3:10). Carrying someone's load creates an unhealthy dependency that is not true freedom, healing, or release at all. It is merely shifting the addiction from one thing to another.

New Creations

When we discover the power of restoring one another without creating an ongoing dependence on us, we will see God show up not only in our own lives but in the lives of the people we are helping. One of the greatest things you will ever experience is God exploding on the scene through you on behalf of someone else. He is faithful and will come through when you do what He has asked you to do. When that happens, you will witness restoration in what had looked like a hopeless situation.

The USS *New York* is an interesting ship. It was made with a symbolic amount of steel salvaged from the World Trade Center after the 9/11 attack. The metal was reconfigured and reused to build a transport ship that carries up to 700 Marines wherever they need to go in order to protect and deliver our citizens from any future attacks. The terrorists of 9/11 had their say, but they didn't have the final say. We rebuilt using what remained, making something brand-new in its place.

Hell has had a say in far too many people's lives as well. Satan has snuck in and damaged individuals, families, and churches. But God has a way of restoring, refurbishing, and rebuilding when we look to Him as the Master Architect of our lives. He can take wreckage in Christians' lives and tweak something here, twist something there, sand something else, and produce something new that will withstand the devil's attacks and help deliver others.

That's what the business of restoration is all about. It is taking broken people and remaking them into new creations who can then go and do the same for someone else. That's how we strengthen the body of Christ and start taking God's kingdom on the offensive in our homes, churches, communities, and nations.

13

COMFORTING
ONE ANOTHER

From time to time I will get a letter in my mailbox addressed to Occupant. My name doesn't appear anywhere on the envelope at all. The meaning of "Occupant" is simple: "We don't care who lives here. In fact, who lives here is irrelevant because we just want to get this to anyone at all."

That's how trouble is sometimes, isn't it? All you have to do is live here on earth, and trouble will discover your address. It doesn't hunt you down personally—it just hunts down anyone at all. If you happen to be in the way, it's your turn for trouble. Life has its ups and downs, ins and outs, pleasures and pains. God is good all the time, but sometimes life certainly isn't.

When I'm preaching about trials, I like to remind my congregation that you are either in a trial, getting out of a trial, or about to head into a trial. The cycle of life simply has a way of incorporating troubles and challenges into our days.

I won't go into all of the details, but I've just had quite a week. My car was stolen while I was at a restaurant with friends. The electrical wiring in my 30-plus-year-old house suddenly started shorting out and needs to be repaired. Two close family members were admitted to the hospital for emergency health issues. And that's just this past week!

So when I talk about trials and troubles, I'm not spouting high-falutin language—I'm speaking from firsthand experience. Jesus said, "In the world you have tribulation." He wasn't kidding. It comes with the territory. But He also said, "Take courage; I have overcome the world" (John 16:33).

Trouble seems to invade every aspect of our lives. It shows up in our relationships, work, finances, homes, churches, health, emotions...In fact, we're hard-pressed these days to truly find smooth sailing at all times in any of the categories I just listed. We live in a fast-paced world with layers of complications and challenges. That's why the "one another" we are looking at together in this chapter is of utmost importance. Without it, we would all remain in a world of hurt.

Paul introduces us to this important concept as he begins his second letter to the church at Corinth. He does this through the repetitive use of the word "comfort."

> Blessed be the God and Father of our Lord Jesus Christ, the Father of mercies and God of all *comfort*, who *comforts* us in all our affliction so that we will be able to *comfort* those who are in any affliction with the *comfort* with which we ourselves are *comforted* by God. For just as the sufferings of Christ are ours in abundance, so also our *comfort* is abundant through Christ. But if we are afflicted, it is for your *comfort* and salvation; or if we are *comforted*, it is for your *comfort*, which is effective in the patient enduring of the same sufferings which we also suffer; and our hope for you is firmly grounded, knowing that as you are sharers of our sufferings, so also you are sharers of our *comfort* (2 Corinthians 1:3-7).

Comfort is obviously a critical concept to Paul and his readers. It serves as the basis for all that he says as he begins this important book on life and living. The Greek word translated "comfort" in these verses may not mean exactly what "comfort" means to us today. When we think of comfort, we often think of things like comfort food or comfort clothes or comfortable cars. We have comfort slippers, comfort cushions, and comfort music to play when we're stressed. We also have comfort oils, candles, and spas.

Of course, Paul wasn't talking about any of those things. He was talking about coming alongside someone to offer help, consolation, and refreshment. Just as someone might offer you a cool glass of water on a hot Texas day, God had offered Paul (and thus the Corinthians) tangible and intangible support.

The supreme biblical Comforter is the Holy Spirit Himself. John 14:16 uses the same Greek term Paul uses so many times in 2 Corinthians. The Holy Spirit's job as the third member of the Trinity is to come alongside and help. He offers not only warmth and solace but also tangible assistance in dire and difficult times. His guidance, instruction, and love provide the comfort we so desperately need.

In 2 Corinthians 1, Paul juxtaposes the comfort with affliction and suffering. Look at the passage again but with a different emphasis:

> Blessed be the God and Father of our Lord Jesus Christ, the Father of mercies and God of all comfort, who comforts us in all our *affliction* so that we will be able to comfort those who are in any *affliction* with the comfort with which we ourselves are comforted by God. For just as the *sufferings* of Christ are ours in abundance, so also our comfort is abundant through Christ. But if we are *afflicted*, it is for your comfort and salvation; or if we are comforted, it is for your comfort, which is effective in the patient enduring of the same *sufferings* which we also

suffer; and our hope for you is firmly grounded, knowing that as you are sharers of our *sufferings*, so also you are sharers of our comfort.

For we do not want you to be unaware, brethren, of our *affliction* which came to us in Asia...

///

When we come to Christ and begin living godly lives in Him, our difficulties can actually increase— but our comfort increases *even more*.

\\

This is why we need comfort in the first place—affliction and suffering exist. They come our way simply because we live on this planet. What's more, those of us in the body of Christ share in His sufferings and endure afflictions that others cannot relate to. Being true disciples of Jesus comes with its own unique set of persecutions and trials (2 Timothy 3:12). So if you were hoping to read a book that says trusting in Christ and serving Him with your life mean you are now immune from trials...well, this isn't that book. The Bible teaches that when we come to Christ and begin living godly lives in Him, our difficulties can actually increase.

But here's the thing—our comfort increases *even more*.

Knowing these things, we should not be surprised by the number of people in the pews next to us at church or in our small groups who are experiencing difficulties in their lives. Nor should we be surprised when our own afflictions increase. Rather, we ought to expect them and prepare our hearts and our minds to share with one another the comfort we receive from God.

Learning How to Be Humble

I'll never forget preaching on this topic not too long ago at the church where I pastor. I was delivering a message on comfort while experiencing a lot of pain. Just a few days before Sunday, my left foot started swelling. The pain had become so bad that on a return flight from a speaking event, I couldn't even walk and had to use a wheelchair. If you know me at all, or if you've read my book *Kingdom Man*, you know it isn't my style to be wheeled around in a chair in public. I was pushed through the airport with my wife walking by my side and my head hung low. It was bad enough that I was in a world of pain, but now I felt embarrassed as well.

Making matters worse, before I preached on Sunday, my doctor fixed me up with an incredibly weird-looking contraption of a shoe. It was half shoe and half sneaker with a big opening for my toes to stick out. It looked awful, and I couldn't wear it without limping.

When I woke up that Sunday morning to get ready to preach, I never even thought about picking out shoes that matched my suit. I was only concerned about being able to walk and being able to preach without being completely distracted by the pain.

Was I humbled by sitting in that wheelchair at the airport while others helped me get where I needed to go? Yes. Was I humbled by preaching two services while limping around in a crazy shoe with the front end cut out? Yes again. But pride is not your friend when you're in distress and need comfort. I needed comfort far more than I needed to look good.

Unfortunately, far too many of us choose another path besides humility as we walk through our trials. We try to hide our pain and pretend our problems don't exist. So instead of getting better, our wounds just become infested and grow. My foot needed the comfort of a specialized shoe and a specialized chair. Had I not used both, the pain in my foot would probably have gotten even worse than it was.

Similarly, when we are going through difficulties and pain in life, we need comfort and support. To deny others the opportunity to assist us, encourage us, and help us get where we need to go in our lives is to delay our own healing. And if we shrink back from comforting others, we can hamper their much-needed healing process too.

Don't let yourself become so concerned with how you look that you make it impossible for others to help you. Don't be so worried about your appearance that you're unwilling to seek out the help you need.

When my foot first became infected, I tried to treat it myself. After all, I didn't want to bother anyone or slow down my own schedule. So I bought some ice and an antiseptic ointment, but those simple remedies didn't solve my problem. It wasn't until I went to the podiatrist that I started to receive the true comfort I needed. He's a professional—he knew what to look for and how to treat what he found.

The first step to receiving the comfort you need in your life is to seek God humbly.

Friend, our God is the God of all comfort. He knows what is causing you distress, and He also knows what you need to get through it and come out the other side victorious. He might send you someone to offer you a word of encouragement or tangible help. He might couple that with the truth of His Word made new to you through the illumination of the Spirit. He might reveal Himself to you in your circumstances as the God of peace—shalom—bringing order and stillness to your emotions as Christ did to the waves of Galilee.

He might do all of those things and more, but the first step to receiving the comfort you need in your life is to seek God humbly. And the first step in comforting others is to welcome and accept them in their humble position.

More Pain Before Comfort

Sometimes a doctor will prescribe a treatment that seems to bring even more pain. Have you ever noticed that some medications have side effects that make you feel even worse? Have you ever required a surgery that left a painful incision? Or, heaven forbid, have you ever had a broken bone reset? Sometimes you may wonder, "Is this healing process worth the pain?" Some people put off going to the doctor or having the surgery they need because they want to avoid the pain. But often, that makes their problem even worse, and eventually they have no choice.

As I sat in my podiatrist's office that day, he afflicted me with more pain than I had when I first walked through his door. He looked at my foot and then pulled out one of the longest, thickest needles I've ever seen. Then he nonchalantly said, "Tony, this is going to hurt."

He wasn't joking. I had to man-up in that office because I wanted to scream. I bit my lip and shook my head as he stuck a big ol' needle into my already throbbing foot. And the pain continued for hours until the medication finally began to do its job. But eventually, the swelling started to go down, the throbbing started to cease, and my layers of affliction began to give way to comfort.

God's ways of bringing comfort to our lives don't always make sense at the start. That's why trust is so important. Perhaps you need to trust Him in your situation right now. Or maybe someone else needs you to encourage them to trust Him in their pain. God's remedies for our afflictions often cause more pain for a while. God isn't being mean. Like a skillful surgeon, He may need to make some incisions to heal the wound. Because of this, comfort can sometimes look confusing. That's why it's all the more essential that we in the body of Christ understand this and give one another the encouragement and insight we need to make it through our times of trouble and trials.

In All These Things

God's Word tells us, "In all these things [trials, struggles, emptiness, pain...] we overwhelmingly conquer through Him who loved us" (Romans 8:37). But do you know something? The most important word in that verse is often overlooked. I must have preached on that verse a hundred times in the last 30 years, but I had never seen this word highlighted the way the Holy Spirit highlighted it for me recently. I was studying this passage in relation to my own life and trials one day, and the Lord had this word leap off of the pages and straight into my soul.

God never promised to deliver us *from* all these things. He has promised that "*in* all these things" we overwhelmingly conquer.

You might think I'm referring to the word "conquer" or "overwhelmingly," but I'm not. The word that stood out to me in that verse is "in." I say it's the most important word because we are often tempted to believe that God has promised to keep us *from* trials, tests, and pains, and when He doesn't, we feel let down, discouraged, or defeated. But God never promised to deliver us *from* all these things. He has promised that "*in* all these things" we overwhelmingly conquer. We experience Him. We receive the benefits and blessings that come only through our deep and meaningful experience of Him.

Friend, this powerful principle needs to be at the forefront of our minds when we are enduring our own trials and when we are comforting those around us who are suffering. Sometimes the pain actually gets worse before it gets better, but that's because God is going to the root of the problem. He's working things out for our good even when we don't have the vantage point we need to understand what's really happening.

I wish I could tell you in good conscience that when you come to Jesus, it won't rain on your parade. Or that when you come to Him, you no longer have to experience difficulties, trials, delays, or other disappointing scenarios. If I could tell you that, or if I could preach that to the people gathered at our church each Sunday, I imagine there would be a whole lot of shouting, clapping, and smiling. But I can't tell you that simply because it's not true.

Yet what I can tell you ought to bring a smile to your face. Whatever happens to you, God promises to use it for your good if you are one of His children and living according to His purpose. When you fully grasp that, it will help you receive comfort during life's bumps, and it will empower you to comfort others.

Your Appointment with God

God longs for a deep and abiding relationship with you. He is dependable, and He wants you to depend on Him. If you are healthy, you probably won't be going to the doctor's office anytime soon. That's because everything in your body seems to be working and doing what it's supposed to do. But when you become sick and don't improve for a long time, you'll probably make an appointment to see your physician as soon as you can.

Similarly, sometimes God allows troubles or trials in your life to get your focus back onto Him. Make Jesus your focus and let His love be your comfort and your strength. Keep your eyes on Him because

He is *for* you. Jesus assures us that He has asked His Father to send us the comfort we need. "And I will pray the Father, and he shall give you another Comforter, that he may abide with you forever" (John 14:16 KJV).

So I can't say that if you come to Jesus or focus on Him, it will never rain. But I *can* tell you that if you will keep your eyes on Him and the promises in His Word, when it does rain, He will be your umbrella. He will be your covering, the shelter that guards your emotions and dreams and the deepest part of who you are. He will protect and nurture your tender core, your spirit. As we learn to keep our focus on the One who promises to cover us, in His covering, we will discover His comfort.

The Lord reminds us through Isaiah of our need for a God-focus in the midst of trials.

> When you pass through the waters, I will be with you;
> And through the rivers, they will not overflow you.
> When you walk through the fire, you will not be scorched,
> Nor will the flame burn you.
> For I am the LORD your God.
>
> Isaiah 43:2-3

He is the God of all comfort no matter
what your afflictions happen to be.

Have you ever seen stunt doubles on television or in movies running around as if they were on fire? They don't get burned because they wear fire-resistant suits. This is similar to what Paul is teaching us in 2 Corinthians 1. He is not saying we will never have to go through fiery circumstances from time to time. He is saying that the God of all comfort will not let us be consumed by the fire around us. He is the God of all comfort no matter what your afflictions happen to be.

You may have a comforter on one of your beds at home. If you do, you know it's designed to keep you warm on cold nights. Comfort from God is also designed to cover you during the cold evenings of life. But in order to receive these benefits from God, you need to allow your pain to drive you to Him. And you need to remind and encourage those around you to do the same. We are to go to God first—not to food, television, entertainment, or spending. When in pain, we need to be reminded of our direct line to the God of all comfort.

How Does God Provide Comfort?

One of the primary ways God brings comfort into our lives is by bringing comforters across our paths. These are other believers who bring comfort and help. God is the God of all comfort, but He often comforts us through others. That's one reason why it is so essential to allow yourself to be a horizontal reflection of Jesus and the Holy Spirit in comforting others. When you do, you carry out God's desires. You reflect God's vertical presence in someone's life by sharing His comfort with them horizontally. God shows up through you!

So when you are concerned only about your own healing, deliverance, and comfort, you block the flow of God's life—His favor, grace, and mercy—through you to others. Disciples are conduits for comfort. Notice the way God's comfort flowed through the Corinthians to Titus and through Titus to Paul.

> When we came into Macedonia our flesh had no rest, but we were afflicted on every side: conflicts without, fears within. But God, who comforts the depressed, comforted us by the coming of Titus; and not only by his coming,

but also by the comfort with which he was comforted in you, as he reported to us your longing, your mourning, your zeal for me; so that I rejoiced even more (2 Corinthians 7:5-7).

Paul lets us in on his personal life by telling us that he was depressed, and then he highlights a key function of the body of Christ. God got him out of his depression by sending Titus. In fact, Paul "rejoiced even more" as Titus told him about the comfort of other people who cared about them as well. It was a chain reaction of sorts. People comforted Titus in his distress, which then empowered Titus to go find Paul in his depression and comfort him. That's how comfort works. As you and I comfort those around us, they are then strengthened to comfort others as well. Before you know it, comfort spreads throughout your home, Sunday school class, small group, workplace, church, neighborhood, community, and more!

Comfort can turn depression into rejoicing, which is something we desperately need in our lives today. We need more rejoicing in our homes, offices, and churches. But that comes about only when committed disciples are willing to be conduits of God's comfort to those around them. If everyone is thinking only about themselves, no one gets comforted.

Channels of Comfort

This is another reason God allows us to go through afflictions. We've seen that He uses our pain to redirect our focus back onto Him. Now we can add that He is also preparing us for the ministry of comforting others in the areas where we have received comfort. He is empowering us to give hope to others in the areas where we have needed hope.

Just a few years ago, I attended a conference and listened to Joni

Eareckson Tada as she gave the keynote address. You may know Joni's story. When she was a teenager, a diving accident left her paralyzed from the neck down. Her testimony that night at the conference had us all spellbound as she shared the trials and tribulations she endures every hour due to her disability. I hung on every word as she spoke of such pain as well as her deep resolve.

At one point in her talk, Joni told us that if she could go back in time and undo that dive, she wouldn't. No one would blame her for saying she would. No one would fault her for wanting to live a normal life without constant pain. But with words laced in determination and strength, Joni said she would not change that day. Why? Because God has used her pain and the lessons He has taught her to bring people to Christ by the thousands and to bring hope to millions worldwide. The comfort she has received from God has become a funnel of life to others.

I admire Joni greatly, and I look forward to the day I see her in heaven fully restored—running, dancing, jumping, and laughing. I won't be the only one there watching. She will be surrounded by those who have been impacted by her courage, comfort, and faith.

When we receive packages at our house marked "fragile," the contents are often surrounded by bubble wrap. Lois removes the bubble wrap and then stores it so we can reuse it when it's our turn to mail something fragile. Just as it had protected something fragile in our lives, we use it to protect something fragile that we give to others.

//

God wraps you in comfort so you can share
that wrapping with someone else later.

\\

In the same way, the Lord wants us to reuse the comfort He has given us in our trials and troubles. He wants us to share it with others as we comfort their fragile hearts and minds in their time of need. He's designed us this way as a means of continuing the cycle of comfort throughout His body. God wraps you in comfort so you can share that wrapping with someone else later. God has a purpose for your pain—to minister to others who are experiencing the same kind of misery you have endured.

Yes, your pain is difficult, and it hurts. I understand that because I've experienced pain myself. But your pain is never just about you. It's about receiving comfort from God so you can give comfort to someone else you can relate to. When everyone in a family, a Sunday school class, a small group, or a church shares comfort with each other, they experience Jesus's presence horizontally. We are His hands and feet to one another. We practice authentic Christianity when God comforts us through each other, empowering us to become ministers of comfort to even more people.

Carpools of Caring

I'm sure you have seen the HOV (high-occupancy vehicle) lanes on urban freeways. Drivers in those lanes can bypass most of the traffic on the highways, but not if they're driving solo. The lanes are available only to those who are carrying passengers. If you go in there alone, you'll get a ticket because the HOV lane is a special-access lane only.

God has a special lane as well. It is restricted to those who connect with others in His name, and it allows them to receive the benefits of a greater experience with Him. It isn't available to Lone Ranger Christians. He didn't establish the community of believers as a long string of solo drivers. You get access to this special vertical lane by ministering horizontally to others. You get blessed because you have made yourself available to be a blessing to someone else.

Do you need comfort in your own life? Then comfort someone else, and together you'll be in the HOV lane to experiencing God's comfort. What you give to others in God's name is what you will receive when you need it. Remember? "Give, and *it* will be given to you" (Luke 6:38). Need comfort? Then give comfort.

Lessons from Clams and Oysters

Clams and oysters can teach us a great lesson about the purpose of our trials. When a grain of sand gets inside a clam or oyster, it causes irritation. This is because the grain of sand is harsh, and it scratches the smooth insides of the clam or oyster. As it continues to cause chafing, the mollusk responds by secreting a substance to smooth the rough edges of the particle. The result is a beautifully rounded and shiny pearl. What began as a nasty irritation to an aquatic creature becomes a beautiful and valuable gem.

God will often use our troubles and pain to reveal the pearl of His presence in our lives.

The lesson of the clams and oysters can help someone when they are going through a terrible trial. They may not be able to remember this lesson on their own when they are in the midst of the pain. That's why the Lord instructs us to comfort one another. We are to be the secretion that surrounds the irritation so that when we come together as brothers and sisters in love, something beautiful can be produced through the pain.

I want to finish our time in this chapter by going back to the apostle Paul and his own words about a time of trial.

For we do not want you to be unaware, brethren, of our
affliction which came to us in Asia, that we were burdened
excessively, beyond our strength, so that we despaired
even of life; indeed, we had the sentence of death within
ourselves so that we would not trust in ourselves, but in
God who raises the dead (2 Corinthians 1:8-9).

Friend, keep in mind who is talking here. This is the apostle Paul,
one of the spiritual giants in the New Testament. This is the only person who ever went to heaven and came back to discuss it. This is the
man God used to write 13 books in the New Testament. When we
talk about Paul, we are talking about a Holy Ghost–filled man of
God, an architect of Christian theology. Even so, this same man tells
us in these verses that he got so depressed, all he could see was death.

One principle we can learn from this is that even spiritual people
can wonder if they are going to make it. Paul said he "despaired even
of life." He couldn't cope anymore; he wanted to give up and throw
in the towel.

*At times we must be stripped of our self-sufficiency
to personally experience God's all-sufficiency.*

Now, if the apostle Paul can get that low, we shouldn't get so worried when we feel that way sometimes or when someone we love feels
that way. Trials and troubles come with the territory of being human.
In fact, God will often use our troubles and pain to reveal the pearl
of His presence in our lives. Paul wrote about a "thorn" in his flesh—
something that was driving him mad. When he entreated the Lord to

remove the thorn, God chose to answer in another way: "My grace is sufficient for you, for power is perfected in weakness" (2 Corinthians 12:9). God chose not to change Paul's situation but rather to allow the pain to continue. God's power would be made perfect through Paul's weakness. At times we must be stripped of our self-sufficiency to personally experience God's all-sufficiency.

Being There for Others

These are tough truths to accept in the midst of pain. These are difficult realities to remember when we, like Paul, are despairing of life due to the trials in our lives. That's why we, as the body of Christ, comfort those in affliction with the comfort we receive from God during our own times of pain. We need to remind each other during those moments that God's grace is sufficient and that He has a purpose for our pain. If we become isolated, we can easily throw in the towel and lose out on the experience of God's goodness in our lives.

We need each other, particularly in times of trouble. Comfort is more than a pat on the back. It's a reminder to hang in there. It's empathy—identifying with the other person because you've been there too. It's giving legitimate help when that is what's needed and you are able. And it's prayer offered in love. Paul wrapped up his talk on his despair with these words of restored hope: "And He will yet deliver us, you also joining in helping us through your prayers, so that thanks may be given by many persons on our behalf for the favor bestowed on us through the prayers of many" (2 Corinthians 1:10-11).

Could it be that God is waiting for you to
focus on someone other than yourself?

One of the greatest illustrations of God's vertical response to our horizontal relationships is from the life of Job. As you probably know, Job had lost everything—his wealth, his children, and his health. Job experienced unimaginable affliction and pain. He eventually received back more than he lost, but notice—when did that restoration occur? Only after Job shifted his focus off of his own pain and onto someone else. We often miss this profound truth in Job's story, so I want to point it out here. In Job 42 we read, "The LORD restored the fortunes of Job when he prayed for his friends, and the LORD increased all that Job had twofold."

The Lord restored Job when Job began living like a horizontal Jesus to his friends. God was evidently waiting for Job to focus on someone other than himself, and when he did, God focused on Job.

Could it be that God is waiting for you to focus on someone other than yourself? I know what you are going through is not easy. I know the troubles you face are challenging and the losses you experience are real. But through that pain, God is developing in you an authentic heart to comfort others, care for them, and love them in His name. Will you take the risk of looking outside yourself and focusing on someone else—being a horizontal Jesus to someone who needs you right now? Maybe that involves offering assistance, a listening ear, or prayer. Whatever the Holy Spirit puts on your heart to do, do it. Because when you comfort someone else, God will comfort you. Ministering to others opens the door for God to minister to you.

Conclusion

Faith with Feet

Everything that exists in the natural world functions according to certain laws God has established—laws by which the world works and runs. Through the process of observation and testing, science helps us identify consistently dependable ways that things work. We can base our lives and work on these laws. We call them "laws of nature," although they are actually the physical laws of God.

But when God invades your natural experience, when He explodes onto the scene, He's doing something *super*natural. He shows up in a way you can't explain. He works outside His own laws to demonstrate that He is not limited by them. God is able to supersede His own laws as He chooses.

Seeing God's supernatural hand at work in your life isn't an everyday occurrence. It requires a heart of faith as well as actions that demonstrate that faith. Without faith, it is impossible to please God. That's why we have taken some time to focus on the "one anothers" in this book.

Living out these "one anothers" isn't always natural for us. Loving, serving, giving, admonishing, restoring...these things require us to put our trust in God, who has promised to reward our obedience to Him. Living as a horizontal Jesus to one another is an act of faith. We need to trust that God will give us the things we need, because we don't always receive those things from one another. We don't always respond to each other the way we should, especially when we're in pain. To live like a horizontal Jesus, we need to pay attention to people's pain in the natural world, but we need to look to God for the supernatural reward we seek—His presence.

This being so, God designed the Christian life to be lived in a group context. The body of Christ is also known as the family of God. God has no only children and no Lone Ranger disciples. If you are seeking God and asking Him to show up and perform a miracle in your life, if you want Him to meet a need or help you in some way, remember how to get His attention. Give, and "it" will be given to you. Whatever you are looking for God to do for you, do that very thing for someone else.

The Power of Many

Throughout our time together, we've been focusing on the importance of what you do for others in accordance with God's principles and precepts in His Word. As we conclude, I want to remind you of a story in Scripture that emphasizes the importance of our collective impact and our collective faith. Sometimes we need more than what one person can provide. Some situations are so dire that the Lord raises up a group of people to come to our aid. Whether you need the support of a group of believers or you are in a group helping someone else, this truth is for you. Much of what God will do in and through us depends on our willingness to do what we can for others.

The story takes place in the book of Mark. Jesus had come back home to Capernaum. The people in that region had heard He was there and gathered where He stayed. So many people had assembled, in fact, that there was hardly any room for anyone else to come. That is where we pick up our story.

> And they came, bringing to Him a paralytic, carried by four men. Being unable to get to Him because of the crowd, they removed the roof above Him; and when they had dug an opening, they let down the pallet on which the paralytic was lying (Mark 2:3-4).

In the midst of Christ's sermon, four men sought to reach him on behalf of someone they knew and cared for who was unable to reach Him on his own. Knowing there was no way to reach Jesus through the crowded room, the men resorted to extreme measures. They carried the paralytic to the roof, opened a hole, and lowered him to the Savior.

This is a popular account in Scripture, and you've probably heard it before, but what I want to point out might be different from what you've normally heard. The story provides a lesson we all need to learn and apply in light of our calling to be a horizontal Jesus to one another.

The paralytic was stuck. He was unable to move forward. He had no control over where he went and how he got there—probably through no fault of his own. He could only lie in a room somewhere and was probably unable to earn his keep. I doubt the paralytic had much hope that his circumstances could change. You've seen people like this, or perhaps you've even been like this yourself. Stuck in a situation or a mindset or an addiction, suffering pain or stress or hardship...it's so overwhelming and has lasted so long, you forget how to hope. You forget how to believe.

The paralytic with no moving legs received the power of eight legs.

That's where the four friends come in. They cared enough for their friend to do for him what he could not do for himself. They knew he couldn't move, so they decided to move him. They loved him enough to change his situation. Yet as they tried to take him to Jesus, they came to a gap. There was a gap between what they wanted for their friend and reaching Christ, who could give it. It was a proximity gap—there wasn't enough room to get to Jesus.

That's when the paralytic with no moving legs received the power of eight legs. These four men demonstrated their compassion for him. They proved their commitment to their brother by doing whatever was necessary to get him to the One who could change his situation. The men took their friend to the roof, dug a hole, and lowered him down to Christ.

Sharing Faith with Others

Jesus's first response is revolutionary, and yet we often skip over it when studying this passage. We read, "And Jesus seeing *their* faith..." (verse 5). Mark doesn't say that Jesus saw the paralytic's faith. He clearly states that Jesus saw the friends' faith. Why is that important? Because when some people have been paralyzed—by hurt, dysfunction in relationships, illness, or any number of things—their ability to have faith has dissipated or disappeared. Sometimes when life has done you wrong, you become too hurt to move forward on your own, and you need some other people who are willing to believe for you. You need to piggyback on someone else's faith.

God responds to others' faith on our behalf.

What an encouraging message—God responds to others' faith on our behalf. We read that when Jesus saw *their* faith, He responded to the paralytic. He forgave the paralytic and healed him—complete restoration.

When the body of Christ is functioning as it was designed to function, people who are paralyzed by their pain are not ignored. People who are stuck are not abandoned. Instead, others in God's family love them, reach out to them, pick them up, and take them to Jesus—even if that means climbing up on a roof, digging a hole, sweating a bit, and carefully lowering them down.

This willingness to sacrifice for one another is rare in our day. Our culture has created a me-mindset. We live for our own gain. Heaven forbid we should be called on to help someone in need. Yet God does not call us to adapt His Word to our culture. He calls us to transform our culture through the power of His Word. And His Word calls us to a life of sacrifice, love, care, concern, action, movement, and love on behalf of one another.

You and I need people in our lives who care about our circumstances and our spiritual condition—people like the four men who served the paralytic. You and I need to be people like that as well. People who will care not only for people's physical circumstances but also their spiritual well-being. Because the four men took the paralytic to Christ, they saw strength return to his legs and forgiveness flood his soul.

God responds to faith with feet.

He does the supernatural when He sees us take steps in the natural world that demonstrate our belief in Him—especially when those steps are on behalf of others who can no longer walk on their own. Now it's your turn to be the hands and feet of Jesus to those around you. Live as a horizontal Jesus, and experience the vertical explosion of God in your life and the lives of those you love.

APPENDIX 1

"ONE ANOTHERS" IN SCRIPTURE

Salt is good; but if the salt becomes unsalty, with what will you make it salty again? Have salt in yourselves, and be at peace with one another (Mark 9:50).

If I then, the Lord and the Teacher, washed your feet, you also ought to wash one another's feet (John 13:14).

A new commandment I give to you, that you love one another, even as I have loved you, that you also love one another. By this all men will know that you are My disciples, if you have love for one another (John 13:34-35).

This is My commandment, that you love one another, just as I have loved you (John 15:12).

This I command you, that you love one another (John 15:17).

Be devoted to one another in brotherly love; give preference to one another in honor (Romans 12:10).

Be of the same mind toward one another; do not be haughty in mind, but associate with the lowly. Do not be wise in your own estimation (Romans 12:16).

Owe nothing to anyone except to love one another; for he who loves his neighbor has fulfilled the law (Romans 13:8).

Let us not judge one another anymore, but rather determine this— not to put an obstacle or a stumbling block in a brother's way (Romans 14:13).

Accept one another, just as Christ also accepted us to the glory of God (Romans 15:7).

Concerning you, my brethren, I myself also am convinced that you yourselves are full of goodness, filled with all knowledge and able also to admonish one another (Romans 15:14).

Greet one another with a holy kiss (Romans 16:16; 1 Corinthians 16:20; 2 Corinthians 13:12).

So then, my brethren, when you come together to eat, wait for one another (1 Corinthians 11:33).

God has so composed the body...so that there may be no division in the body, but that the members may have the same care for one another (1 Corinthians 12:24-25).

For you were called to freedom, brethren; only do not turn your freedom into an opportunity for the flesh, but through love serve one another (Galatians 5:13).

Bear one another's burdens, and thereby fulfill the law of Christ (Galatians 6:2).

Walk in a manner worthy of the calling with which you have been called, with all humility and gentleness, with patience, showing tolerance for one another in love (Ephesians 4:1-2).

Be kind to one another, tender-hearted, forgiving each other, just as God in Christ also has forgiven you (Ephesians 4:32).

Be filled with the Spirit, speaking to one another in psalms and hymns and spiritual songs, singing and making melody with your heart to the Lord (Ephesians 5:18-19).

Be subject to one another in the fear of Christ (Ephesians 5:21).

Do nothing from selfishness or empty conceit, but with humility of mind regard one another as more important than yourselves (Philippians 2:3).

Do not lie to one another, since you laid aside the old self with its evil practices (Colossians 3:9).

Put on a heart of compassion, kindness, humility, gentleness and patience, bearing with one another, and forgiving each other (Colossians 3:12-13).

Let the word of Christ richly dwell within you, with all wisdom teaching and admonishing one another with psalms and hymns and spiritual songs, singing with thankfulness in your hearts to God (Colossians 3:16).

May the Lord cause you to increase and abound in love for one another, and for all people, just as we also do for you (1 Thessalonians 3:12).

Now as to the love of the brethren, you have no need for anyone to write to you, for you yourselves are taught by God to love one another (1 Thessalonians 4:9).

Comfort one another with these words (1 Thessalonians 4:18).

Encourage one another and build up one another, just as you also are doing (1 Thessalonians 5:11).

Encourage one another day after day, as long as it is still called "Today," so that none of you will be hardened by the deceitfulness of sin (Hebrews 3:13).

Let us consider how to stimulate one another to love and good deeds, not forsaking our own assembling together, as is the habit of some, but encouraging one another; and all the more as you see the day drawing near (Hebrews 10:24-25).

Do not speak against one another, brethren (James 4:11).

Do not complain, brethren, against one another, so that you yourselves may not be judged; behold, the Judge is standing right at the door (James 5:9).

Confess your sins to one another, and pray for one another so that you may be healed. The effective prayer of a righteous man can accomplish much (James 5:16).

Above all, keep fervent in your love for one another, because love covers a multitude of sins. Be hospitable to one another without complaint. As each one has received a special gift, employ it in serving one another as good stewards of the manifold grace of God (1 Peter 4:8-10).

Clothe yourselves with humility toward one another, for God is opposed to the proud, but gives grace to the humble (1 Peter 5:5).

This is the message which you have heard from the beginning, that we should love one another (1 John 3:11).

This is His commandment, that we believe in the name of His Son Jesus Christ, and love one another, just as He commanded us (1 John 3:23).

Beloved, let us love one another, for love is from God; and everyone who loves is born of God and knows God (1 John 4:7).

Beloved, if God so loved us, we also ought to love one another. No one has seen God at any time; if we love one another, God abides in us, and His love is perfected in us (1 John 4:11-12).

Now I ask you, lady, not as though I were writing to you a new commandment, but the one which we have had from the beginning, that we love one another (2 John 5).

SMALL-GROUP
LEADER'S GUIDE

This material is adapted from the *Oak Cliff Bible Fellowship Small Group Leaders Handbook*. If you have not yet established a small group in your local church or community, feel free to adapt this overview to fit your own group's needs.

Theology, Vision, Structure of Small Groups
Theology of Small Groups (Why Are We Doing This?)

- God is an eternal community of Father, Son, and Holy Spirit, and He made us in His image (Genesis 1:26). We were designed to live life in community.

- The command to love God is joined with the command to love others (Matthew 22:37-40). That means we will experience more of God when we experience community with others.

- Our church, communities, and world need this. Christian witness is only as powerful as the love demonstrated in community with one another. "By this all men will know that you are My disciples, if you have love for one another" (John 13:35). Small groups help us demonstrate this kind of love to the outside world as we connect in community with one another, grow spiritually together, and serve our church, community, and world together.

The Vision for Small Groups

- To progressively develop small-group opportunities for the purpose of intentional biblical application in a relational context of accountability and connectivity.

- To have a means of measurably identifying the spiritual growth of fellow Christians.

- To develop an ongoing, unified group of well-trained facilitators who will help create and maintain a relational environment for discipleship to occur.

Small-Group Values

- *Connect.* In a small group, we are connected in community by fellowshipping with one another and providing care for each other so that no one stands alone (fellowship).

- *Grow.* In a small group, we grow together by studying the curriculum and applying God's Word to our lives (education) and by responding to God's presence by praying, singing, and praising together (worship).

- *Serve.* In a small group, we serve one another by sharing leadership responsibilities, and we serve together through mission projects for our church, our community, and the world (outreach).

Small-Group Leader Expectations
Job Description

A small-group facilitator is a trained group leader who will oversee an ongoing group of no more than 12 people. The facilitator will encourage connection, growth, and service within the small group by...

modeling an openness to share his or her faith story

facilitating the discussion of the approved curriculum

encouraging participation by all group members

coordinating prayer and care for group members

Expectations

- All small-group facilitators will be growing Christians who have placed their faith in Christ alone for salvation and have a growing, personal relationship with Him. They must also be members of a local church.

- They will commit to a minimum of one year of service (two semesters).

- They will help their group connect with one another in community, grow through the discussion and application of God's Word, and promote an environment of service and care for one another.

- During each semester (fall and spring) they will assemble their group a minimum of twice a month with one additional scheduled time of outside fellowship and one service project.

- They will commit to personally calling each group member at least once a month for encouragement and prayer.
- They will report issues, questions, and challenges that require a pastoral response to the appropriate person.

Make Your First Meeting Great
Goals of the First Meeting

- Rekindle relationships and meet new members.
- Clarify your group's direction, expectations, and commitments.
- Briefly discuss the curriculum you will use.
- Pray that each person will build relationships and grow spiritually.

Contact Your Group in Advance

Contact your group members one week before the first meeting to welcome them to the group and inform them of the location and time of your group.

Three Essential Elements of Your Meeting
Welcome, Mingle, and Talk While You Eat

Studies show that the first seven seconds a person spends in a room can make or break the remainder of their experience in that room. Here are some tips for making your home or meeting place a welcoming environment:

- Greet each person when they arrive.

- Introduce new members to existing members.

- Never let a newcomer sit alone while waiting for the meeting to start.

- Have drinks available when people arrive.

- Play upbeat music as they arrive.

- Provide a clean home or meeting space and turn off your phone.

- Let people know when your meeting will begin in five minutes.

An Agenda for Your First Meeting

Icebreaker. Use the first five or ten minutes to help members get to know each other. If you don't have new members, try sharing things people may not know about you.

Worship and prayer. Singing worship songs is optional, but some groups find this brings them closer together. Prayer is not optional—it's an important component of your group life. There are several ways to incorporate prayer listed below.

- *Popcorn prayer.* Invite people to take turns praying as they are led to do so, and designate one person to close.

- *Groups, clusters, or prayer partners.* Divide the larger group into smaller groups and encourage them to share prayer requests and praise reports with each other.

- *Topical prayer.* As a group, choose one topic to pray about.

- *Written prayers.* Consider praying the Psalms together. Take turns reading them aloud.

Covenant. This is one of the most pivotal small-group tools to set the tone for your group.

- Review the small-group covenant in detail (see the end of this appendix).
- Highlight what it means to make one's attendance at the group a priority. Remember that attendance affects the cohesiveness of the entire group.
- Think outside the box. What else does the group want to commit to? Maybe your group will also covenant to be transparent or to hold each other accountable. This is the perfect time to clarify some of the group members' expectations.

Curriculum. You have a lot of ground to cover in your first group meeting. Do not push the time schedule; rather, let the meeting have a natural flow. But for the sake of establishing a routine, take some time to highlight the curriculum you have selected. If time does not permit that you go deeper, assure the members that your normal routine will allow for more conversation and more application of the Word.

Small-Group Meeting Time Allocation

Each session will last between 1.75 and 2 hours. With 12 participants in each group, it is important that facilitators learn to manage their group time. Below is a typical agenda. Please note that this will not be consistent with every group meeting.

Pre-meeting, greeting, and eating: 10 minutes

Icebreaker: 10 minutes

Worship and prayer: 20 minutes

Curriculum: 60 minutes

Wrap-up: 15 minutes

Maintaining Confidentiality

Small groups provide a community experience that includes intentional biblical application in a relational context of account-ability and connectivity. One component that helps accomplish this vision is confidentiality. Confidentiality is simply the ability to trust each other within the group. This is a vital part of the small-group covenant because it creates opportunities for everyone to discuss issues without fear that they will be shared outside the group. This level of trust means that people are free to share what is on their heart without experiencing a spirit of negative judgment. No one should share sensitive material with anyone outside the group. There are three important reasons why confidentiality is so important to the life of a small group.

- Confidentiality builds trust
- Confidentiality encourages confession
- Confidentiality protects against gossip

Issues to Guard Against in Small Groups

- a group member whose issue or problem is overtaking the group

- a group member who is disruptive to the life of the group—draining its resources, using the group as a personal business network, and so on
- unhealthy relationships forming within the group
- conflict and disagreements between group members
- a group member who clearly and consistently violates Scripture, bringing shame on the name of Jesus Christ

Establishing Healthy Boundaries

Your small group may encounter difficult situations that may be beyond the capacity of your group, such as...

emotional or mental-health issues requiring professional therapy

bitterness or hostility toward a church or its leaders

death or chronic illness

debilitating financial hardship

contentious divorce

This issues are beyond the boundaries of normal small-group life and should be referred to a pastor.

Group Covenant
The Purpose of Small Groups

Small groups provide a community experience that includes intentional biblical application in a relational context of accountability and connectivity. Group members will meet together for the purpose of connecting, growing, and serving together.

Structure

1. My group will meet _____ times a month.

2. My group will meet on (day of the week)
   _____ from
   (month) _____ through
   (month) _____.

3. The group sessions will begin at (time) _____
   and end at _____.

4. We will meet at (location) _____
   _____.

5. We will be studying (topic) _____
   _____.

6. We will covenant together to meet at least once per
   semester for fellowship outside of our regular group time.

7. We will also choose a service project and commit to
   serving together at least once per semester.

Values or Ground Rules

Attendance. We will make the group meeting a priority by attending all meetings and arriving on time. If we cannot attend or will run late, we will contact our group facilitator in advance of the meeting.

Participation. Our group will value the full participation of every group member. We will prepare for each meeting by studying the lesson in advance. We will listen attentively to each group member without interrupting them or carrying on separate conversations.

Confidentiality. For authentic community to form, we must be able to trust each other in the group. This means that issues discussed within the group will not be shared outside of the group.

Connectivity. Our group will value the building of relationships among group members. This means we will commit to pray for the other group members on a weekly basis, follow up on needs that are shared within the group, and seek to hold one another accountable to grow in our walk of discipleship.

Commitment. I commit to uphold the group values reflected in this group covenant.

Signature _____

Date _____

ABOUT DR. TONY EVANS

Dr. Tony Evans is founder and senior pastor of the 9500-member Oak Cliff Bible Fellowship in Dallas, founder and president of The Urban Alternative, chaplain of the NBA's Dallas Mavericks, and author of *Destiny* and *Victory in Spiritual Warfare*. His radio broadcast, *The Alternative with Dr. Tony Evans*, can be heard on more than 1000 outlets and in more than 130 countries.

The Urban Alternative

Dr. Evans and The Urban Alternative (TUA) equip, empower, and unite Christians to impact *individuals, families, churches,* and *communities* to restore hope and transform lives.

We believe the core cause of the problems we face in our personal lives, homes, churches, and societies is a spiritual one. Therefore, the only way to address them is spiritually. We've tried political, social, economic, and even religious agendas. It's time for a kingdom agenda—God's visible and comprehensive rule over every area of life—because when we function as we were designed, God's divine power changes everything. It renews and restores as the life of Christ is made manifest in our own. As we align ourselves under Him, He brings about full restoration from deep within. In this atmosphere, people are revived and made whole.

As God's kingdom impacts us, it impacts others—transforming every sphere of life. When each sphere of life functions in accordance with God's Word, the outcomes are evangelism, discipleship, and community impact. As we learn how to govern ourselves under God, we transform the institutions of family, church, and society according to a biblically based kingdom perspective. Through Him, we are touching heaven and changing earth.

To achieve our goal, we use a variety of strategies, methods, and resources for reaching and equipping as many people as possible.

Broadcast Media

Hundreds of thousands of individuals experience *The Alternative with Dr. Tony Evans* through daily radio broadcasts on more than 1000 radio outlets and in more than 130 countries. The broadcast can also be seen on several television networks and online at TonyEvans.org.

Leadership Training

Kingdom Agenda Pastors (KAP) provides a viable network for like-minded pastors who embrace the kingdom agenda philosophy. Pastors have the opportunity to go deeper with Dr. Evans as they are given biblical knowledge, practical applications, and resources to impact individuals, families, churches, and communities. KAP welcomes senior and associate pastors of all churches.

Kingdom Agenda Pastors' Summit progressively develops church leaders to meet the demands of the twenty-first century while maintaining the gospel message and the strategic position of the church. The Summit introduces intensive seminars, workshops, and resources, addressing issues affecting the community, family, leadership, organizational health, and more.

Pastors' Wives Ministry, founded by Dr. Lois Evans, provides counsel, encouragement, and spiritual resources for pastors' wives as they serve with their husbands in ministry. The ministry focuses on the KAP Summit, which offers senior pastors' wives a safe place to reflect, renew, relax, and receive training in personal development, spiritual growth, and care for their emotional and physical well-being.

Community Impact

National Church Adopt-A-School Initiative (NCAASI) prepares churches across the country to impact communities by using public schools as the primary vehicle for effecting positive social change in urban youth and families. Leaders of churches, school districts, faith-based organizations, and other nonprofit organizations are equipped with the knowledge and tools to forge partnerships and build strong social-service delivery systems. This training is based on the comprehensive church-based community impact strategy conducted by Oak Cliff Bible Fellowship. It addresses such areas as economic development, education, housing, health revitalization, family renewal, and racial reconciliation. We also assist churches in tailoring the model to meet the specific needs of their communities while simultaneously addressing the spiritual and moral frame of reference.

Resource Development

We are fostering lifelong learning partnerships with the people we serve by providing a variety of published materials. We offer booklets, Bible studies, books, CDs, and DVDs to strengthen people in their walk with God and ministry to others.

For more information,
a catalog of Dr. Tony Evans's ministry resources,
and a complimentary copy of
Dr. Evans's devotional newsletter, call

(800) 800-3222

or write

The Urban Alternative
PO Box 4000
Dallas, TX 75208

or visit our website at

TonyEvans.org

More Great Harvest House Books
by Dr. Tony Evans

A Moment for Your Soul

In this uplifting devotional, Dr. Evans offers a daily reading for Monday through Friday and one for the weekend—all compact, powerful, and designed to reach your deepest need. Each entry includes a relevant Scripture reading for the day.

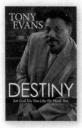

Destiny

Dr. Evans shows you the importance of finding your God-given purpose. He helps you discover and develop a custom-designed life that leads to the expansion of God's kingdom. Embracing your personal assignment from God will lead to your deepest satisfaction, God's greatest glory, and the greatest benefit to others.

The Power of God's Names

Dr. Evans shows that it's through the names of God that the nature of God is revealed. By understanding the characteristics of God as revealed through His names, you will be better equipped to face the challenges life throws at you.

Praying Through the Names of God

Dr. Evans reveals insights into some of God's powerful names and provides prayers based on those names. Your prayer life will be revitalized as you connect your needs with the relevant characteristics of His names.

Victory in Spiritual Warfare

Dr. Evans demystifies spiritual warfare and empowers you with a life-changing truth: Every struggle faced in the physical realm has its root in the spiritual realm. With passion and practicality, Dr. Evans shows you how to live a transformed life in and through the power of Christ's victory.

30 Days to Overcoming Emotional Strongholds

Dr. Evans identifies the most common and problematic emotional strongholds and demonstrates how you can break free from them—by aligning your thoughts with God's truth in the Bible.

30 Days to Victory Through Forgiveness

Has someone betrayed you? Are you suffering the consequences of your own poor choices? Or do you find yourself asking God, *Why did You let this happen?* Like a skilled physician, Dr. Tony Evans leads you through a step-by-step remedy that will bring healing to that festering wound and get you back on your journey to your personal destiny.